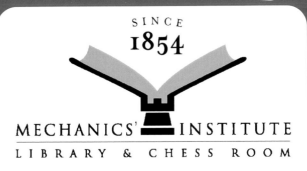

the art
and power
of being
a lady

Noelle Cleary
&
Dini von Mueffling

Atlantic Monthly Press
New York

Published simultaneously in Canada
Printed in the United States of America

FIRST EDITION

Library of Congress Cataloging-in-Publication Data
Cleary, Noelle.
  The art and power of being a lady / Noelle Cleary and Dini von Mueffling.
      p.   cm.
  ISBN 0-87113-793-3
  1. Women—United States—Social conditions.   2. Women—United States—Conduct of
life. I. Von Mueffling, Dini.   II. Title.
HQ1421 .C58 2001
305.42'0973—dc21   2001018853

Design by Julie Duquet

Atlantic Monthly Press
841 Broadway
New York, NY 10003

01 02 03 04   10 9 8 7 6 5 4 3 2 1

Dini:
For my daughter, Tati, who in her grace, dignity, and laughter is already a lady

Noelle:
For my mother, Maria Luisa Cleary, who shows me every day what *dignity* is all about; and for my beloved father, John Francis Cleary, who taught me the meaning of the word *grace*.

Contents

What Time It Is • Keeping Her Cool • A Few
Words on Cursing • Smoking Courtesies • The
Limits of PDA • Grooming at the Table • Meeting,
Greeting, and Getting Along • Off-Limits Topics •
Gossip • A Lady Need Not Suffer Through
Offensive Remarks • Phone Rules to Live By • Last
But Not Least: E-Etiquette

The Power of Style • A Lady Is No Slave to Fashion •
It's Not About Money, Honey • Letting Her Assets
Shine • The Art of Dressing Appropriately • Building
Her Wardrobe • The Finishing Touches Count •
Portrait of a Lady's Basics: A Working List • Style
Trademarks • Lady-style Icons: Audrey, Katharine,
and Jackie • The Best Accessory Is Confidence •
Home Style

The Power of Friendship • When the Going Gets
Tough • When the Going Gets Good • Telling It
Like It Is • Her Friends and Lovers • Friendship
Takes Effort • The Authors' Turn to Gush

100 who are ladies

Whether it's their authentic style, their social consciousness and contributions, or their undeniable grace and dignity, all of these women have that certain something that compels us to call them ladies. To save paper, we've condensed the list to one hundred. But, believe us, there are hundreds more where they came from!

Madeleine Albright
Christiane Amanpour
Jennifer Aniston
Brooke Astor
Angela Bassett
Candice Bergen
Ingrid Bergman
Carolyn Bessette Kennedy
Cate Blanchett
Sandra Bullock
Carol Burnett
Kitty Carlisle Hart
Rosalynn Carter

Katie Couric
Sheryl Crow
Matilda Cuomo
Blythe Danner
Chelsea Clinton
Jamie Lee Curtis
Edwidge Danticat
Catherine Deneuve
Princess Diana
Gloria Estefan
Chris Evert
Edie Falco
Jodie Foster

Ruth Bader Ginsburg
Elizabeth Glaser
Whoopi Goldberg
Katherine Graham
Mia Hamm
Emmylou Harris
Audrey Hepburn
Katharine Hepburn
Carolina Herrera
Anita Hill
Faith Hill
Lauryn Hill
Katie Holmes
Holly Hunter
Gwen Ifill
Jacqueline Kennedy Onassis
Caroline Kennedy Schlossberg
Billie Jean King
Dr. Mathilde Krim
Christine Lahti
Queen Latifah (Dana Owens)
Geraldine Laybourne
Rebecca Lobo
Shoshanna Lonstein
Sophia Loren
Andie MacDowell

Sarah McLachlan
Julianna Margulies
Oseola McCarty
Linda McCartney
Michael Michele
Alanis Morissette
Toni Morrison
Kathy Najimy
Jessye Norman
Suze Orman
Gwyneth Paltrow
Sarah Jessica Parker
Rosa Parks
Jane Pauley
Paloma Picasso
Natalie Portman
Miuccia Prada
Anna Quindlen
Queen Noor
Leah Rabin
Bonnie Raitt
Dana Reeve
Ann Richards
Julia Roberts
Eleanor Roosevelt
Isabella Rossellini

Susan Sarandon
Pat Schroeder
Donna Shalala
Brooke Shields
Maria Shriver
Liz Smith
Lesley Stahl
Julia Stiles
Meryl Streep
Da Aung San Suu Kyi
Sheryl Swoopes

Emma Thompson
Uma Thurman
Christy Turlington
Barbara Walters
Venus Williams
Serena Williams
Oprah Winfrey
Reese Witherspoon
Michelle Yeah
Jessica Yu
Paula Zahn

first prologue

By Dini von Mueffling

THE IDEA for *The Art and Power of Being a Lady* came about several summers ago. A friend said, in talking about a woman he had dated, "She was like you. A lady." I wasn't sure how to take this. After all, he was fifty, but I was only thirty.

A lady, I thought to myself. Am I pleased to be called that? I was just getting used to being called *ma'am* in the grocery store, a moniker I'd been coming to accept since I was now the mother of small child. Still, it often made me turn around to see which matron behind me the deli man was speaking to.

Lady. To whom could I ascribe the term? Audrey Hepburn, of course, and Jacqueline Kennedy Onassis. They were icons of a bygone era, though. I thought some more. Oprah Winfrey, whom I admire for myriad reasons. Julia Roberts came to mind, as did Anita Hill. I included Madeleine Albright. Lauryn Hill. Julianna Margulies. Women who are modern and gracious. The more I thought about it, the more I realized that I considered it a compliment to be called a lady. I was pleased because I realized that if my friend thought I was a lady, I had done something to earn it.

I also quickly saw that I had recoiled from the connotations that came with the word—connotations that I didn't believe were me at all. Was a lady a Generation-X, working, single mother? Reflexively and, I know now, inaccurately, I thought of a lady as someone high-society, even frivolous, with a disposable income and time on her hands, who knew how to set a table perfectly. But that was not the image of the women I conjured up when I really thought of the word's meaning. After all, wasn't Jackie O also what I was—single mother, career woman, and modern?

Lady also reminded me of the familiar refrain that rang through my home as a child: "Dini, behave like a lady!" What my mother meant, whether she was whispering it with a wink or as she gritted her teeth, was to mind my manners and be well behaved—to be like her. That was fine when I was in grade school, but when I came of age in the eighties and got my first job in journalism at seventeen, I thought that version of lady life, that of a fifties-era wife and mother, was sorely outdated. It was only recently that I realized the message was the same even if the context was different.

So what made a woman a lady? Dignity and grace, for sure. Self-confidence, independence, a sense of right and wrong and the strength to act on it, a sense of social responsibility, humor, style, and good manners. Above all, consideration of others. In the go-go eighties, when barreling ahead was all that mattered, it was hard to remember to mind my manners—and *why* it was important to use them—in a newsroom filled mainly with gruff men and women fighting for their piece of the action. This was a scene being played out nearly everywhere for all my female friends. But there was power in being a lady, in rising above the fray, in not trying to be one of the boys *all* the time, in using femininity not to manipulate but to bring a different, important perspective to the table.

I was sold—and I wanted to share this notion with others. I called my closest college friend, Noelle, whom I think of as very different from me but every inch a lady, and asked her what she thought. Before we knew it, we were writing *The Art and Power of Being a Lady*.

second prologue

By Noelle Cleary

IN MY upbringing, the word *lady* didn't play a very large part. Perhaps because my mother is Italian, it didn't hold as much social weight as it did for English-speaking women.

My mother's word for how to behave was *dignitá. Dignitá* was less about table manners and social order and more about being a woman who spoke up for herself, had self-respect and integrity, was honest and gracious. And she taught us about all of those things without ever using the word *lady*.

As a young mother coming into her own in the 1960s, she was in the throes of the women's movement. She attended consciousness-raising meetings and hung on every word uttered and written by one of her heroes (to this day), Gloria Steinem. This made for interesting dinnertime conversation, especially since my father was twenty years her senior and, to put it simply, was and always would be stuck in the attitudes of the 1950s. So as my father discussed for the umpteenth time having played in the Bing Crosby Invitational Golf Tournament in his glory days, my mother waxed on about the merits of women in the armed forces and *Roe v. Wade.*

Even with all the changes that were taking place, my mother's highest priority was always to set a positive example for her children. Of course, she taught us the basics—like table manners, how to conduct ourselves among adults, and most importantly, how to handle others' social transgressions gracefully.

What I remember most about what she taught us was the frequency with which she used the word *respect.* We were told not only that every single person deserved respect and consideration, but that we should expect the same from others. She also made a special effort to ensure that my sister and I knew our opinions were just as important as any man's, and that we deserved the same kinds of opportunities as boys. Sometimes she hosted her own mini-revolutions on our behalf: for example, I was the first girl to play on my town's Little League baseball team, much to the monumental embarrassment of my poor brother, whose team I played on.

Many of our neighbors made unkind comments about my parents' age difference, my mother's accent, and the fact that she went to work in an era when most mothers still stayed home. (Some foolish souls had the audacity to mimic her to her face, to which she usually responded with a humoring smile and an offhand comment in French—one of the three languages she speaks fluently. That usually managed to change the subject.)

I knew at my core that the standards she was setting forth were about how she and I saw ourselves in the world, and how we wanted the world to see us as well. They were manifested in the example she set as a mother (she is unrelentingly supportive and involved), as a wife (she was my father's most dogged advocate and, in the end, the best nurse anyone could have prayed for), and as a working woman (I still consider her one of the best negotiators on the planet).

In retrospect, I realize my mother was teaching me how to be the best person I could be. That is, she was teaching me how to be what I now fondly refer to as *my* kind of lady. Which is why when Dini called me two years ago about writing this book, I didn't have to think twice.

introduction

AS WE enter the new millennium, there are more women than ever
in the workforce, in positions of power, being elected to public
office, and playing central roles in major industries. We admire
those who are at the very apex of their careers, women who have
beaten the odds and remained ladies. Our most-admired Hollywood star is not a male action hero but the genteel leading lady
Julia Roberts. Our number-one talk show host, Oprah Winfrey,
is not a sleaze peddler but a paragon of compassion and social
consciousness. And two of the best athletes in the world are teen-
age sisters Venus and Serena Williams—ladies who have revived
the game of tennis with a supernatural combination of strength,
grace, and style.

Aside from their remarkable achievements, these women also
shine for the way they conduct themselves in many aspects of
their lives—with grace, dignity, and a constant awareness of how
their behavior impacts others. They're living proof that *how* we
succeed is just as important as success itself.

Unfortunately, though, in this time of enormous prosperity

and infinite possibilities, we've become socially lazy. These women are very much the exceptions, not the rule.

In our culture today, we place an increasingly high premium on professional success, earthly possessions, and outward appearance—at almost any price. The media gives us what we allegedly want: stories ad nauseam about celebrities' new looks, new mansions, new lovers, and trips to rehab and jail (not necessarily in that order). And let's not forget those chart-topping TV shows like *Who Wants to Marry a Millionaire?*, *Survivor*, and *Temptation Island*—programs that unabashedly glamorize greed and betrayal. While some conscientious public figures try valiantly to shine their spotlights on people who do good, we are still far more fascinated by the tawdrier side of life. The culture of fame and consumption is upon us.

Then there's our private lives. Women have made great social progress in the last forty years (and it's nothing to sneeze at!). With the positive change though also came some confusion: it seemed that anything at all went . . . for men as well as women. What kind of world are we living in if the most intimate and personal details of an affair between an intern and the leader of the free world can become the subject of after-dinner conversation for everyone on the planet . . . when we have been told to behave like men in the workplace to get ahead and are still expected be the perfect combination of Martha Stewart and Pamela Anderson when we get home (who *wouldn't* be confused?).

The advent of feminism brought many welcome changes, from a woman's right to work and receive equal pay to her being able to choose whether or not to be a mother. It also gave us the opportunity to select our partners based less on their ability to provide and more on their character. These changes called into question many basic ways in which men and women interacted on a daily basis, leaving many of us uncertain whether it was gracious or insulting to open a door for a woman. We applaud the early feminists—we wouldn't be where we are today without their struggles for equality—and questioning those behaviors pointed out something important: that how women *respond* to them is more significant than the tradition that mandated them. But we believe that it's now safe to evaluate some of these old chestnuts from the vantage of the progress we've made. We feel it's silly not to trust women to be able to tell the difference between a courteous gesture and being treated like a helpless maiden.

There's also the simple fact that the pace of life is a lot faster. In this day of "Be all that you can be," "Every woman for herself," and "She who dies with the most toys wins," there's no denying we've lost sight of some of the more noble attributes that used to be held in high regard, particularly among women, such as: dignity, discretion, courtesy, humility, and social consciousness. Qualities that the women we hold up as examples today possess in abundance. Qualities that our mothers were speaking of when they told us to behave like ladies.

* * *

We know what you're thinking: why on earth are we dusting off such a seemingly prissy, nineteenth-century term to describe our ideal for the twenty-first-century woman? Some of our closest, smartest friends balked at the word when we first told them about this book. But we thought more about it. The word *lady* is supposed to be the female equivalent of the word *gentleman.* Though most of our male friends aren't landed gentry, they know what we mean when we call them gentlemen, and they know it's the highest of compliments. Then we thought of the women who come to mind when we think of the word *lady.* Women of style *and* substance—women we admire and who inspire us. The more we thought about it, the more we realized that no other word captured exactly what we were after. Whether a woman is Jane Doe or as famous as Katie Couric or Gwyneth Paltrow, living gracefully, as a lady, brings her admiration and respect from others—and that's where the *power* comes in.

In fact, the word *lady* has already begun making its own comeback. *Ladies First* is the title of a hit song and best-selling advice book by rap artist, talk show host, and actress Queen Latifah. In describing soccer star Mia Hamm and her World Championship U.S. Women's Soccer teammates, sports commentators frequently used the word *ladies,* referring to their remarkable off-the-field conduct as well as their playing. Foot Locker created an ad campaign of women athletes captioned with one word: *ladylike.*

These examples illustrate perfectly the kind of ladies we mean. So if you still think a lady is a snob, a prude, or a doormat, try telling that to Queen Latifah. Which makes the need for this book apparent—with the word *lady* being tossed out as much as it is, we feel it needs to be defined once and for all in a way that reflects our independence, our new challenges, our achievements, and our modern attitudes toward relationships, sex, work, parenting, and our places in the world.

In other words, we wanted to make the word *lady*—and the values it stands for—relevant again, and show its importance for *all* women. So we did some research of our own. We interviewed and surveyed women of all ages, professions, backgrounds, and ethnicities about what being a lady means to them—at work, in relationships, at home, in their communities. We created an online survey and forwarded it to our friends, asking them to e-mail it on. Nearly two hundred women took part: women from locales as diverse as New York City, Los Angeles, New Orleans, St. Louis, and Seattle, as well as a multitude of rural and suburban areas. Our survey respondents were single mothers, former welfare recipients, actresses, politicians, massage therapists, newscasters, writers, artists, lawyers, teachers, librarians, students, activists, secretaries, social workers, and more. What they all had in common was that they answered "yes" to the survey's first question: "Do you consider yourself a lady?" Their thoughtful and candid responses play a large part in the book.

Being a lady is not about having the best designer clothes;

drinking a wine spritzer instead of what you really want (like a Guinness on tap); batting your eyes and playing coy instead of using your brains and wit to flirt; taking your boss's shortcomings lying down; or pretending to be fulfilled by less than enough.

It *is* about standing up for what you believe in, being true to yourself, showing an appreciation and regard for others, and seeing beyond the superficial junk we are fed every day of our lives. It's a tall order, but certainly not impossible, as you will read.

When you leave this world, you are not going to be remembered for your fabulous wardrobe, how many cars you had, or your ability to still fit into the jeans you wore in high school. You're going to be remembered for what you contributed to your world, however small or large. You're going to be remembered for being a real *lady*.

So go ahead and turn the page. But check your preconceived notions at the door. Our kind of lady is not what you might expect.

ONE

the portrait of a lady . . . today

*I think ladies expect people to treat them with respect
and in turn that's exactly what those people get back.
In order to be considered a lady, I think you have to
treat people with grace, sensitivity, and dignity.*
—PAULA ZAHN

WHAT MAKES a woman a lady? Is it a concept worth reclaiming?
Do you have to be born a lady, or can you become one?

Over the last year, we've asked many people what the word
lady meant to them. They told us: grace, dignity, consideration,
independence, confidence, self-awareness, humor, respect,
compassion, social awareness, and style. Combine all that with
working or being a student or a parent (or all three), being a
good spouse or partner, being a good friend, and oh yes, trying
to be good to yourself. Now it sounds impossible. However, a
lady is not daunted. She's not perfect and she knows it. But as
Candice Bergen put it, "I think you can't help but fall short of

your goals sometimes. But even falling short indicates a certain amount of awareness of how one ought to behave. And that, in and of itself, is the essence of what being a lady is all about."

Many people believe that this kind of awareness and savoir faire is impossible to learn. But we believe a lady is made, not born. While she may have her mother to thank for setting a great example, a lady earns her stripes through her behavior—and that's something that's entirely up to her: not by merely dressing appropriately to an occasion (although she does that), or writing thank-you notes (she does that, too), but by conducting herself in a way that takes into consideration the world around her and how she interacts with it. She does it in little ways, such as taking care to say please and thank you to the person she buys her coffee from each morning. Or by refilling the paper tray in the copy machine when she's done. Or by extending herself to those less fortunate than she. Or by mentoring a younger employee at her job.

While the stress and pressure of daily life make it seem hard to accomplish more than the task at hand, by stopping to think of others, a lady maintains perspective. Before she knows it, the initial effort and discipline become second nature. Which is when a woman becomes a lady.

Being a lady is an attitude. It's about being content with ourselves and confident in our abilities. It's about feeling good and about looking good, too. But mainly it's about *doing* good.

More than anything, a lady *knows* herself and is thus able to see *beyond* herself to what's really important. A lady takes the long view—she isn't swayed by zeitgeists or the more permanent communal lowering of standards. She holds herself to a higher standard because she respects herself, and she knows in the fast pace of modern life there's no substitute for life's simple values— self-awareness, the strength she derives from good friends, the rewards of doing her job well, living richly, and giving something back to the world. That's the art of being a lady.

While each lady has her own special balance, there are some things all of them share.

GRACE

*Grace is one of the first words that comes to mind when
I think of a lady. She is filled with confidence, so much
that she has no need for ostentation, grandstanding,
one-upmanship, or self-promotion. A lady is at peace
with herself, so everything she does springs from the
purest of intentions.*

—JADA, CONCORD, NH

Grace is difficult to define, but we know it when we see it. It's a habit of mind that prizes calm and self-assurance over impulsiveness; it's the poise to respond to what the day brings and the perspective to share one's blessings. It's what makes a lady stand out from the rest.

They Know It When They See It

She's really a smart girl . . . who has been raised with a lot of confidence and self-esteem, so she seems older than she is in many ways. . . . She has a natural *grace* that doesn't make her seem as if she's of her generation.

—Actress Susan Sarandon on actress Natalie Portman

I really dig how she walks around. It's like she doesn't care how she looks or what she projects. And it's not that she doesn't care . . . it's that she's not affected, I guess. And that gives her *grace*.

—Rob Gordon (played by John Cusack) in the film *High Fidelity*

It's through everyday acts that a lady exhibits grace. She's the one to smooth over a disagreement between two people; the one who handles a work crisis successfully without letting pressure get to her; the one who, no matter how frustrating someone can be, takes a breath and counts to ten instead of losing control.

Pictures of Grace

At just twenty-one, Chelsea Clinton has proven the embodiment of a lady. In her, we see someone who has exhibited unwavering grace in the face of her father's travails as well as her mother's controversial run for U.S. Senator. Whether acting as her mother's partner on the campaign trail or her father's travel companion throughout the world, she has always been genuine, polite, kind, dignified, and good-humored. Another former first daughter, Patti

Davis, wrote this about Clinton: "I'm learning from Chelsea Clinton. I've found inspiration in the effortless grace that a girl half my age has brought to an intimidating challenge."

Tennis powerhouses Serena and Venus Williams have often exhibited grace beyond their years. When they tour, they always make a point to reach out to the fans in the countries where they are competing. At the 1999 French Open, at which the sisters won the doubles championship, they addressed the crowd in perfect French, for which they received boisterous cheers and a standing ovation. It's this extra effort that sets them apart and makes them role models to whom young girls may aspire.

Grace under pressure is the truest mark of a lady. No one personifies this attribute better than Madeleine Albright. As the first female secretary of state, Albright was always in the public eye as she steadfastly worked to foster peace among world leaders. At the beginning of

A Gossip with Grace

Gossip columnist Liz Smith is an unfailing forgiver of foibles, a believer in second chances, and a champion of the underdog. Well aware of the power she wields on her page, she uses newsprint not just to dish but to enthuse about a worthy play, a cause, or even a person she admires. While one might think a columnist's reputation would suffer from being known as a softy, her generosity and graciousness not only distinguish her from her peers but work in her favor. When celebrities have "confessions" to make or a story to break, Miz Liz is the one they turn to first because of her unwavering sense of fairness.

her tenure, Albright jetted around the globe reaching out to heads of state—sometimes to countries that had never even had a U.S. cabinet member visit—establishing relationships over the long term rather than scrambling to build them when a crisis arose.

Another woman who almost always comes to mind when we think of grace is the late Princess Diana. She touched a nerve in people worldwide through the compassion and concern she exhibited for those less fortunate than herself. Much more than a maker of perfunctory gestures, Diana used her position to spotlight children's issues, AIDS, and the eradication of land mines, causes that so often victimized the voiceless whom she knew she could help.

Through their grace, these ladies have shown us that even the smallest selfless gesture—especially one that is unexpected—can affect others in enormous ways.

Gentle Reminder

Consummate lady Sarah Jessica Parker (who doesn't quite play one in *Sex and the City*) chose the word *grace* as the screen saver on her cellular phone, to remind her "to be good to people."

DIGNITY

Dignity is intimately related to grace. But while grace becomes apparent largely in how we interact with the world, dignity is much deeper within us. Dignity is having great respect for ourselves—our thoughts and strengths (and weaknesses). It is by respecting ourselves that we earn respect from others. In acting with dignity, we act deliberately. Because we respect ourselves and take our lives seriously, we make our own choices in how to live. While all of us make silly choices sometimes, dignity is an inner voice telling us to get serious. Dignity is what allows us to walk through the world with our heads held high.

Anita Hill showed great dignity during her ordeal testifying at Supreme Court nominee Clarence Thomas's confirmation hearings. In the face of haranguing senators determined to discredit her, Hill was calm and confident. Her dignity underscored the gravity of her testimony.

Another lady who epitomized dignity in the face of tragic loss is Leah Rabin. After the assassination of her husband, Israeli prime minister Itzhak Rabin, she immediately called for calm in her country rather than retaliation. Though most others would have crumbled, she had the grace and dignity to make sure that no further violence would erupt in her husband's name.

Dignity and grace go hand in hand. One almost always goes with the other. They are a lady's armor and her hallmarks.

A LADY LAUGHS . . . EVEN AT HERSELF

Lest all of this seem a little daunting, let's remember: a lady never forgets to laugh—and has enough perspective to laugh at her own mistakes. In 1998 Christine Lahti won a Best Actress Golden Globe award for her role in *Chicago Hope*. Unbeknownst to her, the award was to be presented just moments after she had exited the auditorium to go to the ladies' room. Her name was announced and she was nowhere in sight. For what seemed like an eternity, aides searched high and low for Lahti. A few moments later she appeared on the stage, overjoyed and flustered. Instead of ignoring the whole debacle and thanking the usual list of agents and producers, she began her acceptance speech by profusely apologizing to her mother. The entire auditorium broke into hysterics.

A lady knows that life is too short to take it all so seriously. After all, there's no point in nurturing our dignity and standing on principle if we aren't having any fun!

When we asked our survey respondents to name the three qualities they valued most in themselves, a sense of humor was at the very top of the list. A lady's sense of humor enables her to cope with the challenges of life, gives her perspective, and makes her good company. She knows that laughing strengthens her spirit and goodwill.

Gossip columnist Liz Smith has a wonderful sense of humor, which she often turns on her column subjects as well as herself. When we wrote to Smith, asking to interview her for this book, she wrote back, "I got a kick out of your letter and of course would talk to you about ladies in general. Not being one myself, I am an expert." (Naturally, we disagree, particularly since she wrote, typed, and signed the letter herself! What a gracious lady.)

When a lady knows herself and is comfortable in her skin, she can easily laugh at herself. As NBC News correspondent Maria Shriver wrote, "I find when I have an accurate picture of myself—and accept and appreciate where I am in my life and where I still want to go—that's when I have the perspective and attitude that allows me to enjoy myself and have a good laugh."

A LADY IS PROUD TO BE HERSELF

All of this may sound like you have to be born a lady, but nothing could be further from the truth. It's all about balance and self-esteem—qualities by no means limited to ladies but which they have in abundance. A lady has dignity and grace because she believes in herself and is proud of her accomplishments. She accepts compliments graciously and knows the difference between self-esteem and self-absorption. She knows that her achievements are the products of her hard work and commitment—no matter how great or small they are. So while she would never boast, she doesn't downplay the esteem she earns.

In our survey, we asked ladies what they thought were their most significant achievements. The majority of respondents pointed to their capacity to handle the challenges of modern life. Their wide spectrum of replies never mentioned just one thing but always reflected doing well at several things and achieving a graceful balance.

- "My thirty-one-year marriage to a wonderful man, my three incredible children who are loving and engaging human beings, and my past seven years as a counselor in a private day school."—Audrey, Weston, MA
- "Raising my son alone from age two, completing a triathlon and half-marathon, and starting a foundation to raise funds for girls and sports."—Pamela, Old Greenwich, CT
- "Leaving my abusive marriage, swallowing my pride and going on welfare, putting myself through school, getting a good job and going to the welfare office to let them know I no longer needed their services!"—Dana, Brockton, MA

The necessary partner to pride is humility. Humility is what keeps our feet on the ground, enabling a lady's gracious attitude. Sometimes humility means letting others shine, as Candice Bergen did in 1998. Having won the Emmy for Outstanding Lead Actress in a Comedy Series five times in seven years, after her last season, she discreetly took herself out of the running so that other actresses might be recognized for their work. Bergen, the sentimental favorite, knew that one more Emmy wasn't going to make a huge difference to her, but to another actress, it could mean the world. After all, a lady like Bergen didn't need the nomination to measure her achievement.

THE TWO Cs: CONVICTION AND COURAGE

The quality I admire most is courage. Specifically, the
courage to care more about truth than presenting a
face or an opinion that someone else wants to hear. To
sound hokey, I admire the courage it takes to be
oneself.   —*NICOLE, NEW YORK CITY*

A lady's courage stems from the strength of her convictions. She lives her life in a manner that's consistent with her moral, social, and ethical beliefs. She isn't afraid to be in the minority when she takes a stand on something important to her.

A lady may not necessarily view herself as brave. As one survey respondent wrote, "I don't think anything I've done is particularly courageous, although others might think so. I just try and rise to the occasion." This is precisely what a lady's courage and conviction is about: trusting her instincts and doing the right thing. Not for accolades or for popularity but to do what she knows she should—whether it means leaving an unhealthy relationship, leading an intervention for a friend with an alcohol or drug problem, blowing the whistle on an employer for unfair business practices, or giving up a lucrative job to pursue a more fulfilling path in life.

Our poster girl for conviction is actress Natalie Portman. While the media try to lump her in with the many young actresses promoted as sex symbols, she persistently shies away from being labeled. She will not allow herself to be photographed in a sexually provocative manner because she wants to set a positive example for young girls, and she weighs seriously the image she projects in a movie. Portman even initially turned down her role in the mother-daughter film *Anywhere But Here* because there was a love scene with nudity that she felt was gratuitous. Costar Susan Sarandon—another lady of conviction—said she wouldn't make the movie without Portman, so the scene was cut.

Courage is not always easy; every lady has fears to tackle before she goes out to slay dragons. But whether it takes surrounding yourself with friends or it's just a personal bridge to cross, courage is essential to being a lady. Our survey respondents each had her own tale of courage: whether she wrote of talking a young girl down from a bridge, representing herself in court against the two men who raped her, or of rescuing a woman being beaten by her husband, each of these women had done something incredible. And yet because of her powerful convictions, each felt that her action was not a choice at all but something she *had* to do.

Speaking of courage and conviction, Oprah Winfrey seems to have an endless supply! Not only has she always shared her personal stories (the sexual abuse she suffered as a young girl, the child she gave birth to as a teen, her struggles with her weight) in the hopes of helping others, she has always striven to rise above. A few years ago, when her talk show was rated number one, she decided to change her format and stop airing sleazy stories—thereby separating herself from the bulk of the talk show world. Sending a positive message to her viewers was more important to Oprah than a few extra rating points or the risk of losing ad revenue. She had enough conviction to do what she knew was right. Her courageous approach has only increased her popularity and confirmed her as a role model for women and men alike.

PRACTICAL MATTERS

In the old days, it was fine for a lady to be a damsel in distress or a princess whose castle moat protected her from having to deal with the nuts and bolts of life. But a modern lady is nothing if not practical. She prides herself on being self-sufficient, independent, and competent. In fact, the dignity and grace with which she lives her life are derived from pride in her ability to manage the little things that make life run—be it the ins and outs of car and home maintenance, her finances, health, or psyche. This isn't to say that a lady doesn't ask for help if she needs it (she'd never be like one of those stubborn guys who won't ask for directions). She just uses her head and tries to manage on her own first.

A LADY TAKES CARE OF HERSELF, INSIDE AND OUT

My recipe for health? Water, sleep, and self-acceptance.

> —*DANA REEVE, ACTRESS, WRITER, AND WIFE OF CHRISTOPHER REEVE*

Not just for herself; but also for those who care about her, a lady takes care of herself. Our health is something we have control over, to a large degree, and we should take it seriously. A lady knows this, so she tries to learn from what others before her have gone through. Here's what a lady does to stay healthy:

- She gets regular checkups, including a pelvic exam once or twice a year (as her doctor advises), dental visits, and eye exams.
- She learns how to do and gives herself regular breast self-exams.
- Health is her most important asset, so she's comfortable discussing her health concerns with her doctors. (If she's intimidated, she makes a list in advance.)
- She learns about her family's health history and knows her risk factors.
- She pays attention to her body. If a health issue arises, she takes care of it as soon as possible. If she cannot afford a doctor or does not have health coverage, she finds out which free clinics provide the best care and utilizes them.
- When she's really ill or going through a hard time, she calls on family and friends to give her support—just as she'd do for them.
- She makes an effort to eat right and exercise regularly, knowing that doing so doesn't just make her live longer but also makes her feel (and look) better.

A LADY TAKES TIME OUT FOR HERSELF

A lady's definition of health goes beyond the physical. It's also emotional and spiritual. Even when she's balancing multiple roles, a lady's secret to maintaining her equilibrium is to take time for herself. For any one of us leading busy lives, this seems easier said than done. But whether it's getting a manicure or a massage, going for a walk solo, taking a trip to a museum, or renting a movie and watching it uninterrupted, a lady knows a little break is essential to recharge her batteries. Taking time out for herself benefits her and everyone around her.

A Great Lady Shows Us How It's Done

At ninety-nine, Brooke Astor does yoga every morning. Astor has often said that the secret to her longevity and health has been moderation in eating and drinking. She is proud of having never had a face-lift: "A doctor once told me not to lose or gain too much weight and to use a sensible cream and I would never need plastic surgery."

One of our survey respondent's biggest indulgence was "getting up at 5:30 A.M. to garden and letting my husband do breakfast for the kids." Taking care of ourselves is about the pause that refreshes—and sometimes the little present for yourself that gives you joy and rejuvenates you to face whatever's next. If shoe shopping is your way of relaxing, we say go for it (in moderation).

SHOW HER THE MONEY AND SHE'LL SHOW YOU THE MEANING OF SAVVY

A lady knows that in this day and age, she has to be smart about money. She knows at any given time approximately what she has, what she can do with it, what she owes, and how she's going to pay for it. If at all possible, she has something set aside for emergencies. Even if she doesn't work and relies on her partner to pay the bills, she makes sure there's money for her in that equation.

If financial knowledge isn't her strong suit, a lady reaches out and gets educated. Recognizing that she's weak in this area and needs help doesn't make her feel helpless; it motivates her to get with the program. Her goal is to improve the statistic that only 20 percent of women today have set aside enough money for their retirement and the future.

There are many good books available that deconstruct the ins and outs of personal finance. A favorite of ours is Suze Orman's *The 9 Steps to Financial Freedom,* which explains the hows and whys of financial responsibility in a very accessible manner. As Orman (a lady, we might add) writes, financial knowledge is not only a matter of survival but a key to personal empowerment.

HER HOME IS HER CASTLE

A lady learns how to handle the plethora of large and small catastrophes that may arise on any given day at her home, such as a blocked sink, backed-up toilet, testy smoke detector, blown fuse, loose cabinet handle, tape stuck in the VCR, squeaky door-hinge . . . the list goes on.

This is not to say a lady has to be a master plumber, elec-trician, or carpenter—obviously there will be times when a repairperson is the only option. But she makes the effort: she reads her appliance manuals and keeps them handy. Armed with a basic tool kit (makes a great gift!) and at least one book on basic home maintenance (*Home Improvement for Dummies* is a favor-ite of ours), you'd be surprised how much troubleshooting can be done—and money saved.

A Car Is a Lady's Friend

Sometimes we forget how much we rely on our cars to get us to work, to day care, to school to pick up the kids, to the gym, to the store, to the beach on the weekends, and everywhere in between.

While she may not know how to rebuild her engine, or the going rate for a reconditioned alternator, she knows that she needs an oil change every three thousand miles or three months; that washing her car is about getting corrosives like salt off the body, not just making it look shiny; and the proper pressure for her tires. And we applaud any lady who can change her own oil or replace an air filter!

A lady also knows to ask questions of people who know more than she does about cars, and she takes someone with her to

Just for Fun

When we polled our ladies, we asked them some peculiar questions that they answered like troupers. Here are some fun facts about our survey respondents . . .

99% can read a map
96% can swim
91% can balance a checkbook
86% can check their oil
78% own toolboxes
77% can drive a stick shift
74% can program a VCR
68% can do the Heimlich maneuver
67% can do their own taxes
67% can hem pants
61% can knit
47% can speak a second language

the garage if she has one of *those* mechanics. She comparison-shops and isn't afraid to ask questions.

All of what we have described in this chapter springs from a lady's number-one asset: an undeniable sense of self-worth. It's the foundation for her dignity and grace, her capacity for compassion, strength, and forgiveness.

A lady values herself not based on how others see her but rather from reaching within. As Julia Roberts put it, quite succinctly, in a *Rolling Stone* interview: "[W]hat it really boils down to, ultimately—which is corny and textbooky—[is] if you don't truly care for yourself, if you don't find yourself that interesting, then you'll never believe anyone else who claims they do."

We couldn't have said it better ourselves.

TWO

manners that matter

Manners are the exercise of the
imagination on behalf of others.
—ELIZABETH BOWEN

IN THE days of yore, manners were about always holding the door for a lady, lifting your pinkie as you sipped your tea, and knowing how to make a place setting with five forks. But in the modern age, expectations have become looser, and it's certainly not the end of the world if you don't know what that small angled knife is for (fish), you get the door for yourself, or you occasionally put your elbows on the table.

However, with all this relaxing of the rules, it appears some of the other, more important courtesies of daily life have also gone the way of the eight-track tape player. How else can we explain those individuals who yell into their cell phones in restaurants, shove past you to get into the subway, or neglect to wave "thank you" when you let them into your lane so they can make their exit?

These are fast-paced times. We all have too many things to do and not enough time to do them. And yes, sometimes we forget the common courtesies and civility that help to separate us from monkeys. Which is why we've compiled some original thoughts on manners for the new millennium, and how a lady conducts herself in this world of cell phones, e-mail, and instant gratification.

We apologize in advance if you're curious about how to eat an artichoke (*very* carefully), or the proper wording for a formal wedding invitation; we recommend you consult the useful and time-tested etiquette books by Letitia Baldrige, Emily Post, and others for the answers to those questions. We've chosen to focus on those courtesies that capture what manners mean to the *modern* lady.

Needless to say, the following guidelines should not be used to judge others. A lady realizes that she often sets an example for others and accepts that responsibility with grace. After all, she herself may even have an occasional lapse, so she extends her respect for others to give them the benefit of the doubt. Getting steamed about someone's failure to be courteous in a small way is, in our opinion, a waste of precious time and energy.

A LADY'S FAVORITE WORDS: *PLEASE* AND *THANK YOU*

It's easy in this self-involved world to forget about the people who make everyday life run smoothly—the man who prepares our bagels, the woman who steams the soy milk for our chai lattes, the teen who bags our groceries, even the person who holds the closing elevator door for us. Taking others for granted is all too common, but a lady makes the effort not to. She knows someone's efforts to be helpful, kind, and courteous should never go unacknowledged, and that taking a moment to recognize and appreciate others comes back to her in spades.

Our maxim: go overboard with niceties like *please* and *thank you*. No one's ever been offended by those simple words, and heck, they're so darned easy to say!

Since we hardly need to explain the proper usage of the word *please* (except to point out that it is preferable to start a sentence with "please" rather than "I need you to"), we're going to move on to *thank you*—if you please.

Before Miss Manners Came George

George Washington's volume of rules on civilized behavior was, according to historians, jotted down while he was acting general of the U.S. Army during the Revolutionary War. He learned a great deal from the dignitaries he encountered while he served as general, and according to both his contemporaries and his biographers, Washington valued good manners and painstakingly cultivated his own brand of formal courtesy. (Example: "In disputes, be not so desirous to overcome as not to give liberty to each one to deliver his opinion and submit to the judgment of the major part . . .") All of Washington's *Rules of Civility* are as applicable today as they were two centuries ago. Maybe that's

→

35

why one of our favorite leading ladies, Julia Roberts, told an interviewer that it's the book she carries with her wherever she goes, and that she aspires to live up to every single one of George's rules.

Thank you is one of the most-used phrases in a lady's lexicon. She knows it goes a long way and, delivered in earnest, makes everyone feel good. When people go out of their way to be accommodating and thoughtful, a lady lets them know that she has recognized their efforts. It doesn't have to cost a thing except the time it takes for the words to leave her lips. And a big look-'em-in-the-eyes smile doesn't hurt, either.

Little Things

Claire: "Every afternoon I get a cappuccino from this little place downstairs from my apartment. I like it with skim milk, lots of foam, cocoa on top—I'm a pain. At Christmas I gave the women cards with little tips to thank them for their great service. It made me feel good. It made them feel good. And I've noticed that the other people who go in and just bark their order don't get the kind of attention that I do. It just goes to show you how even the smallest niceties can go a long way."

GRATUITY

The art of the tip has gotten increasingly confusing in recent years, especially when tip cups seem to sprout up in places they've never been before—such as Starbucks or Dunkin' Donuts. A lady knows there are those who must not be overlooked in showing her appreciation, and tipping is one of those things it is pretty hard to overdo.

After all, the word *tip* is short for **to** **i**nsure **p**romptness. Here are some guidelines on who always gets tipped.

- In a restaurant: the waiters, the coat-check person; the maître d' or hostess for service above and beyond the call of duty
- Anyone who provides a personal service such as haircuts, manicures, massages, shoe shines
- Taxi drivers
- Hotel workers, from bellhops to cleaning ladies, and even the concierge if he or she is particularly helpful
- Doormen, cleaning people, building staff, and anyone else who makes our daily lives run smoothly should get a gift or extra money at the holidays

A lady knows that she is not expected to supplement the income of a service-industry provider who is paid an hourly wage that doesn't incorporate tipping (such as Starbucks), or to tip in places where it is expressly discouraged.

The "when" and the "how much" of tipping is discretionary, but if you're really not sure, the 15-to-20 percent rule never left anyone feeling underappreciated.

GIVING GIFTS

Another way a lady shows gratitude is with a gift. She may do this when money is inappropriate (she wouldn't tip a schoolteacher) or if she wants to make a more personal gesture. A lady keeps her gift in proportion to her income. For example, if she's as rich as Oprah Winfrey, she might fly her dedicated staff in a private jet to New York for a shopping spree at Bergdorf Goodman. But for those of us who aren't quite there yet, a homemade pie, a book, or a bottle of bath salts with a note is just as thoughtful.

WRITE IS RIGHT

I write thank-you notes. I don't e-mail them, I write them on stationery. Whenever people take the time to extend themselves, I think it's important to acknowledge that. And it's a way to maintain connections as we see each other and talk to each other less. —CANDICE BERGEN

Despite the convenience of e-mail and Instant Messenger, the best way to show appreciation is still with a handwritten thank-you. A lady does it immediately if not sooner. It doesn't matter if it's on a postcard she's picked up at a kiosk outside the ladies' room at her favorite pub, or on engraved Crane's stationery. She just does it. While the next day is ideal, we say better late than never.

One way to make the task easy is to keep the necessary ingredients on hand—a box of different blank cards, some stamps, and a pen are all you need. We like to pick up cool cards whenever we spot them. You never know when you'll be compelled to jot a quick note of thanks for a great party, a thoughtful gift, or the time and ear someone gave to help heal post-breakup wounds.

KNOWING WHAT TIME IT IS

About 80 percent of the respondents to our Web survey listed tardiness as a pet peeve. We had to chuckle when we discovered soon thereafter that half of those same ladies confessed to having problems with punctuality. (Some were even brave enough to admit that they're usually more than fifteen minutes late!) It's never too late to mend your ways, and here's how Tracey, in Seattle, Washington, reconciled her own chronic lateness: "My parents were always ten minutes late to pick me up from school, meetings, or sports practice. It drove me crazy. But worse than that, I never developed a sense of *other* people's time. One thing that has helped me become more conscientious is the realization that when I'm late, I'm stealing time from other people. And stealing is *never* ladylike."

Being punctual makes you a better candidate for success. When I am on time, I'm relaxed, more confident, and more likely to get what I want and need.—*FATIMA, BROOKLYN, NY*

The lady who just can't get it together sets her watch ahead, writes down an earlier time in her appointment book, or creates self-punishment if she's late (i.e., no chocolate for a week, or worse, no shoe shopping for a month). Being on time for dates and appointments shouldn't be that difficult. But as we all know, nobody's perfect. When a lady is late, she always has a good excuse (and no matter how tempting, it's not a made-up one) and is always profoundly apologetic.

KEEPING HER COOL

A lady never screams in what she says or how she says it.
—LESLEY STAHL

Sure, every lady has a bad day here and there: the dog eats her favorite shoes, her hair decides to go frizzy on her before an important meeting, her Christmas bonus doesn't quite cover all the presents she's already bought. . . . And then there are those needless aggravations brought on by others, like the guy in the car ahead who drives twenty miles an hour, the checkout gal who goes on a coffee break in spite of the long line of customers, the person who shoves past you into the subway car just as the doors close.

In spite of the countless daily opportunities to blow her stack, a lady reminds herself that the world is not conspiring to annoy her, although it may feel that way. Regardless of how bad a day she's had or how incredibly rude someone else has been, she knows there is absolutely no excuse for taking out her frustrations on innocent bystanders. Everyone knows what it's like to be on the receiving end of misdirected wrath. Our kind of lady can contain her steam, no matter how trying some moments get. As one of our survey respondents offered: "I've found that when I get inordinately angry about a situation beyond my control, it's usually something about myself that's making me mad. At the risk of sounding New Agey, taking some deep breaths and figuring out what's really eating at me usually does the trick."

A Few Words on Cursing

I find being foul-mouthed kind of unattractive. . . . So I just
try and avoid the truck driver in me.   —UMA THURMAN

We all experience moments when, unfortunately, the only words that seem appropriate (or at least the first ones out of our mouths) are the kind that would make our grandmothers blush. However—and this is important—a lady knows the limits. While some ladies might think this outrageous (or just plain wrong), we believe cursing is one of those guilty pleasures that, used wisely and thoughtfully, has the kind of impact necessary in some situations—if for no other reason than to let off steam. A curse word never killed anyone. However, that's still no reason to let loose with vulgarity in every other sentence.

If you are one of those rare people who never lets a bad word pass your lips, good for you. But for the rest of us, the time and the place for occasional vulgar language is:

- Among friends and acquaintances with a similar verbal tolerance
- Alone in a car and to yourself (not to the jerk who just cut you off)

- When you absolutely, positively can't help yourself (always excuse your language immediately if you're in the company of others whose profanity threshold is unknown)

When a lady does *not* use vulgar language:

- In front of children, regardless of whether their parents swear
- At work
- In front of people who don't ordinarily hear such language
- So often that people start thinking you have a very limited vocabulary

As Candice from Metairie, Louisiana, put it, "I think a lady is allowed to curse like the proverbial sailor under the proper circumstances; but let me add that a lady is able to define the proper circumstances."

SMOKING COURTESIES

Smoking is one of those touchy subjects that can get the nonsmoker and smoker equally worked up. Public health laws (some would say thankfully) removed some of the uncertainty. But for that gray area that remains:

- A lady never smokes in the company of nonsmokers without asking permission first. If someone protests, a lady does not get angry or indignant. Rather, she excuses herself and goes outside. Furthermore, she doesn't light up in someone's home without the permission of the host and other guests.

- She *never* smokes in close proximity to children, particularly infants.
- A lady is never caught dead dropping her butt on the ground or out of a car window. She holds on to it until she finds a proper receptacle.
- She does not give cigarettes to minors, no matter how uncool they make her feel or how desperately they plead.

If a nonsmoking lady encounters a presumptuous smoker, she handles the situation not with a lecture but by politely saying, "I'm afraid your smoke is bothering me." (And in a restaurant, she is more than entitled to ask a waiter or hostess to step in, particularly in the face of cigar smoke.)

THE LIMITS OF PDA

There's nothing better than that ethereal feeling of being in love (or infatuation, or good old-fashioned lust). Sometimes one is overcome by these feelings and indulges in PDA (public displays of affection), but ladies know that anything more than the occasional brief kiss and hand-holding falls under the category of too-much-information for the rest of us. While we excuse the hormonally challenged adolescent who likes to grope his or her beloved in the hallway at school (and everywhere else), everyone else is old enough to know better. Here are three activities we believe should be reserved for private moments: passionate, lost-in-the-moment kissing; touching of any body part ordinarily clothed; and any other behavior that causes others to feel the need to avert their eyes or quip, "Get a room."

GROOMING AT THE TABLE

The dinner table is not a vanity, nor should a lady's vanity be displayed there. If she has to retouch her makeup, apply lipstick, comb her hair, or adjust her bra straps or pantyhose, she goes to the ladies' room . . . and goes to town.

MEETING, GREETING, AND GETTING ALONG

Sleep not when others speak, sit not when others stand,
speak not when you should hold your peace, walk not
when others stop.
　　　　　—*GEORGE WASHINGTON*, RULES OF CIVILITY

Manners are more than just rules of etiquette, of course. They're also about social interaction and the challenges that we face when dealing with different kinds of people—all with as much grace, dignity, and diplomacy as we can muster. Because our modern lady possesses a healthy amount of self-confidence, she is not often flustered by the social indiscretions of others. (This is not to say that some of us haven't been temporarily thrown off by some lewd or rude remarks.) But because she conducts herself with a generous amount of regard for other people, she expects the same from the company she keeps.

In our survey, many ladies vented about what they observed as a lack of civility today. (And we had to concur.) So at the risk of preaching to the choir, we thought a basic refresher might be in order.

A lady always looks people in the eye when speaking to them. It's a sign of respect and consideration and also inspires confidence from others. (Noelle: "My mother used to tell me, 'Never trust someone who doesn't look you in the eye when speaking to you.'")

She shakes hands upon meeting someone new (unless it is against that person's custom). In the case of friends, she may choose to kiss or hug hello unless the setting is a business event where this would be inappropriate.

A lady does not interrupt when someone else is speaking (no matter how brilliant her point may be). She knows her turn to speak will come.

OFF-LIMITS TOPICS

Back in the day, many subjects were considered off-limits in mixed company: sex, religion, politics, money, illness, bodily functions, occupations, the looks of anyone present (especially to note changes), the possessions of anyone present, divorce, world suffering. These rules were created in large part because many of these discussions were considered unseemly for women. Hence the after-dinner cigar and brandy hour for men, with tea and sherry for the women in another room. These taboos also served another function: to allow conversation to focus on matters other than daily life, such as art, music, and literature.

While we still discourage discussions of controversial topics in the company of people whose feelings are unknown, it's not necessarily the crime against civility it was in the past. After all, it's natural to be curious where others stand on important issues. And some thrive on the electricity of a good debate. (How many of us *haven't* talked about the 2000 presidential election debacle ad nauseam?) However, a dinner party or other social event is not the appropriate occasion to engage people's politics, morals, and social tolerances. For one thing, debate is work, and while some people love such verbal exercise, others despise it. For another, a social gathering is not the place for an emotional and highly personal exchange—the sort that is better left to a private, one-on-one conversation.

So a lady gauges her company. If curiosity takes her conversation in the direction of possible conflict, once she gets an idea of the other person's stance, she will try to politely change the subject. However, she knows it's okay if she's among friends and trusts that the subject at hand will not deteriorate into a bitter argument (either because they all agree or they know how to disagree gracefully). But a lady makes sure the conversation doesn't devolve into a self-congratulatory exchange, which is boring at best and at worst, self-serving gum-flapping.

GOSSIP

Be not hasty to believe flying reports to the
disparagement of others.

       —GEORGE WASHINGTON, RULES OF CIVILITY

Gossip is an area in which a lady sets herself apart. While idle talk about the affairs of others may seem innocuous, sometimes it isn't. Once words are spoken, there's usually no way to undo any damage they may cause. So if she realizes a conversation would make her uncomfortable if she were the subject, a lady just doesn't go there. If she's the thick-skinned type, then she is even more careful. As the grandmother of a friend always said, "When in doubt, ask yourself: Is it true? Is it kind? Is it necessary?" If not, a lady thinks twice.

Let's face it, gossiping makes people look nosy . . . and unladylike. Recognizing that exploiting other people's personal lives is often driven by the desire to be popular, a lady, of course, rejects the temptation.

It's so easy to discourage others from malicious gossip by saying something gentle, such as "Let's not talk about Jane without her being here." Or just change the subject. It's really that simple.

A Lady Need Not Suffer Through
Offensive Remarks

It happens all the time. Some joker decides a social situation is the perfect opportunity to try out some of his or her off-color or otherwise offensive jokes on a new and unsuspecting audience. Or worse, they're not jokes at all, but his or her intentional disparagements of a particular group. We say no lady should have to sit quietly through the prejudiced or tasteless diatribes of others. More importantly, a lady knows there are ways to handle an offensive person that will quickly end his or her nonsense and spare others any further discomfort. For example:

- A wry grimace and pointed exit from the conversation work to silence all but the most obtuse offender and serves two purposes: it lets everyone know that she does not subscribe to the speaker's attitudes, and she no longer has to listen to the drivel.

- Repeatedly correcting offenders can slow them down enough to lose their train of thought altogether—the perfect opening for someone to change the subject.

- Earnestly explaining the offense is another clever tactic. In the words of the inimitable Judith Martin, Miss Manners: "There's nothing like the threat of a sociological lecture to encourage casual bigots to change the subject."

- A lady might take the offender aside, say that his or her language is not universally appreciated, and suggest that he or she save that kind of talk for the company of confirmed like-minded people.

A lady doesn't take on the task of changing someone's mind in one fell swoop. She knows these things will not be unlearned in a day. But if she spends time with this person (work, social necessity), her mere presence will be a constant reminder and hopefully give him or her pause before spouting off offensive remarks in the future. (It's worked for us!)

Finally, a lady does not risk being misconstrued as concurring with an offender by saying or doing nothing. She does not betray her own beliefs, and she is never a coward. (And need we say a lady does not subscribe to bigotry of any kind?)

PHONE RULES TO LIVE BY

Call waiting and cell phones can be very handy, making keeping in touch more convenient. Unfortunately, they've brought with them countless woeful opportunities to forget good manners. In our survey, nearly 50 percent of our respondents thought that phone manners were in desperate need of a revival. Cell-phone etiquette in particular was a red-hot manners topic. While busy people are now easier to get hold of, the fact that phone communication is possible nearly anywhere does not mean that it's appropriate. Too often people forget they are not the only people in the room—whether they're on a cell or regular phone. For that reason, we offer the following phone rules to live by:

If a friend is pouring out her heart on the phone, a lady does not take another incoming call. (They don't call it call *waiting* for nothing.) If she can't help herself, or is expecting an important call, she lets the second caller know up front she's on another call, and she won't make her friend wait more than a moment (ten to fifteen seconds) while she takes the incoming call.

If she's in the middle of a meeting, interview, dinner, etc., a lady does not take a phone call unless she's expecting something urgent—such as a call from her baby-sitter or the update from her best friend's delivery room. She knows it's important to let the people she's with know they have her full attention.

When she enters a public building (whether a restaurant, bank, or grocery store), a lady will 1) shut off her cell phone, 2) turn it to "vibrate," or 3) turn down the ringer so that only she can hear it.

If a lady absolutely must take a call while at dinner or anywhere other people are congregating, she always excuses herself and goes outside. (Okay, if she's in an airplane before takeoff, that's not so easy. So a lady considers the people next to her and keeps the call brief and to a murmur.)

The proper volume of a lady's voice when speaking on a cell phone (or just speaking in public) is one that can be heard only by her and the person to whom she is speaking. If she's outside and there is traffic noise, she will go somewhere she can hear herself. She does not start yelling into the phone, assuming the rest of the world doesn't mind learning her business—not to mention that it's impossible to respect the confidentiality of the person she's speaking to.

Because a lady cares about her safety and that of others, if she spends a lot of time in the car, she will purchase a hands-free device so she can keep her hands where they belong—on the steering wheel.

If someone doesn't abide by these rules, we cannot take responsibility for the glares and nasty under-the-breath comments people will make in her direction. (Especially in Seattle, we've discovered.) We've also noticed that if you're in Los Angeles or New York City, the rules seem regrettably loose. But as we like to say, one million wrongs don't make a right.

LAST BUT NOT LEAST: E-ETIQUETTE

The age of e-mail has ushered in a whole new mode of communication. (Who would've thought we'd someday be expressing moods with colons, semicolons, and parentheses?) With its light-speed immediacy, e-mail has replaced many

Response Time

A time-related pet peeve that was shared by many in our survey was not calling people back. A lady knows it's not that hard to pick up the phone or type a quick e-mail letting someone know she got a message, even if she doesn't have time for an extensive conversation. It's a common courtesy we should all get in the habit of doing. In that vein, one anonymous respondent wrote: " I was careless in not returning a friend's phone call for a few weeks, and she had called to invite me to her impromptu wedding and I was one of the few she had asked!"

traditional forms of connection, from the phone to the letter, memo, or fax. While we may get more things done faster, we have lost no small measure of civility in the process. But a lady always approaches e-mail with her own set of guidelines, none of which sacrifices speed for substance.

A lady makes sure the tone of her e-mail is appropriate. While e-mail often makes phone calls unnecessary, a lady never forgets that it can't communicate her tone of voice, so she will take the time to make sure it is clear and avoid misunderstandings.

Upon receiving an e-mail, she answers back, even if it's just to say "Thanks for the info." It's frustrating not to know if an e-mail was received, even if the recipient viewed it of little consequence. (Obvious exceptions: jokes and chain e-mails.)

A lady uses forms of address when initiating contact. (She wouldn't write a letter or use the phone without addressing the respondent.) She includes her name at the end, knowing that not everyone knows her e-mail address on sight.

She takes care to use proper grammar, punctuation, and spelling, as if writing a letter, knowing if she makes errors, she is diminished in the eyes of her reader.

She is aware that e-mail is not confidential and is retrievable and easily shareable. Thus she takes care not to send her own or her correspondent's secrets (or anything she would truly mind if someone else read) through cyberspace.

A lady may add a personal touch to her e-mail when appropriate, knowing that it will differentiate hers from the myriad others someone else may be receiving. This may be as simple as an inquiry after the recipient's family or a gentle compliment.

A lady refrains from incessantly forwarding jokes, stories, petitions, or other junk mail that would disrupt her e-friends at work. When she just can't help herself, she marks the subject "not work-related." That will let the recipient know that the message isn't urgent or personal and he or she can read it at leisure.

A lady's good manners not only set the standard for others to follow, they also make whatever environment she is in more pleasant. Two hundred years after our first president wrote *The Rules of Civility,* we still say civility rules.

THREE

a lady's style:

authentic and undisputed

Style is what you make of the face you were born with.
Frida Kahlo, Georgia O'Keeffe, and Anna Magnani—
women who I feel have style, allure, and elegance—did
not submit to any standard of beauty. They defined it.
The beauty I admire most doesn't hide flaws but
underlines our absolute singularity.
—ISABELLA ROSSELLINI

STYLE IS as essential to being a lady as her good manners. It's the perfect combination of the attitude she wears and the clothes she wears with it. Above all, a lady's style is about making it look effortless, uncontrived, and uniquely hers, with confidence and grace.

As designer Miuccia Prada put it, "Though the way you dress is probably the least important thing about you, it's the first thing others see. So, if you dress in a personal, individual way, it probably means that you are very strong, very sure of yourself." Eighty-two percent of our survey respondents said that style was an important element of being a lady.

A lady's style is an expression of who she is and what makes her tick. Think of Audrey Hepburn, whom the world fell in love with in capris and a pixie haircut. Or the Williams sisters in their body-hugging tennis outfits that accentuate every powerful muscle and feminine curve. Or Julia Roberts, always sleek and understated in her trademark look for evening: elegant black dresses accessorized by her knockout smile. While the rest of Hollywood glitters and shimmies, Roberts steals the show by not trying so hard. We see her, not her clothes: a lady who is comfortable in her skin, who likes who she is and wants the world to see her for just that.

A lady's style is as individual as she is. It has nothing to do with how much she spends on her clothes and everything to do with what she chooses to wear and how. It's about putting her best foot forward, whether that foot is wearing a clog, a Manolo Blahnik stiletto, or a high-top sneaker. It's the lady that wears the clothes, not the clothes that wear the lady.

A lady knows that having style gives her power. As actress Sandra Bullock phrased it, "Style is whatever makes you feel however you want to feel at that moment. That's the great thing about clothes. They're like armor."

Lastly, a lady knows that style is about living well and having fun. Rather than viewing getting dressed each day as a chore, she sees it as her way to be creative and illustrate the choices open to her. We are long past the days when women were confined to a uniform mode of dress. Today we can create our own style in just about anything we want to put on. And a lady does just that, with attitude.

THE POWER OF STYLE

I think [style is a] way that women can, on a daily
basis, really express themselves. You can say, "Today
I'm a bitch; today I'm a milkmaid."

—GWYNETH PALTROW

A lady understands the power of style. We send messages through what we wear. Clothes—and jewelry, hairstyles, makeup, and perfume—can bolster us when we're facing adversity or can send someone the hint that we're feeling sexy. They can say "Don't mess with me today" or get us geared up for girls' night out on the town. The individual way a lady wears it all tells the world that she's unique, and that she's decisive and comfortable with herself. She doesn't have major traumas when she gets up in the morning and decides what to wear, because what's in her closet reflects her.

Maybe you like Winona Ryder's vintage chic or Whoopi Goldberg's fabulous dreadlocks. The statement you make through your clothes and hair is the least important one you will make in your life, so have fun with it. A lady is aware of the subliminal messages she sends through her style and knows how to use them.

The spun-candy-pink dress Gwyneth Paltrow wore when she won the 1998 Oscar for Best Actress was the image of sophistication and grace. And that was how she expressed herself, as she talked about how bittersweet the victory was after the death of her grandfather, and her father's serious illness.

A lady's style is about looking right for the moment and in her attitude toward it, whether the moment is the Academy Awards or taking her college finals. Dini: "A high school teacher of mine once gave me some invaluable advice: 'When taking an exam, don't dress down. Dress up, you'll do better.' She was right." Likewise, if you feel more roll-up-your-sleeves productive in jeans—go with it.

A lady's clothes can also express her conviction in times of strife. During Clarence Thomas's Supreme Court confirmation hearings, all eyes were on Anita Hill, whose participation made her the reluctant star. In impeccable suits that underscored the gravity of her allegations, she sent a no-nonsense message. She wrote in her autobiography that she thought carefully about her decision to wear her bright blue linen suit on the day of her history-making testimony. "Do you look like someone who is credible?" she had asked herself. Hill knew that as a woman who "did not conform," every aspect of her would be doubly scrutinized.

Even civil-rights heroine Rosa Parks used her clothes to make a statement. That fateful morning in 1955 when she arrived in court to answer the charge of breaking the law by refusing to give up her bus seat to a white person, she had picked her outfit carefully. In his biography of Parks, Douglas Brinkley wrote:

> *Just about all five hundred of the African Americans who assembled on the steps of Montgomery's city hall that first day of the 1955 bus boycott shared one distinct impression: how elegant Rosa Parks looked in her long-sleeved black dress, with its starched white collar and cuffs, black velvet hat with faux pearls around the top, and straight dark gray coat.*

What Rosa Parks said with her clothes subtly underscored what her refusal to tolerate segregation already had. Parks altered the landscape of racism in this country not with a raised fist but with a dignity that could not be denied.

A LADY IS NO SLAVE TO FASHION

Every season we are bombarded with a new slew of fashion dos and don'ts. A lady, however, sees fashion trends for what they are: fleeting flights of fancy—sometimes fun, sometimes downright unwearable! She knows the next new look has little impact on her personal style.

This is not to say a lady ignores fashion completely. For example, if python is the current rage, a lady might buy a pair of snake-print shoes or a bag for fun. But you won't see her clearing a section of her closet to make room for the subsequent python skirt, jacket, and boots. When she dons something of-the-moment, she makes the look hers—she has no desire to look like a fashion victim. And she knows better than to splurge on ultra-

Sage Advice

Never take on a fashion trend that doesn't flatter or support your figure. You end up spending every second you wear it pulling at your straps, tugging at your skirt, or checking to make sure nothing is popping out.

—SHOSHANNA LONSTEIN

trendy items that she'll doubtlessly toss out because they'll be passé in three months. She's practical, spending money thoughtfully, with an eye toward longevity.

We shine our spotlight on those who buck trends and wear what they love, such as Claire Danes, Candice Bergen, Jodie Foster, Andie MacDowell, Julianna Margulies, Julia Roberts, and Uma Thurman. They exemplify style, originality, and confidence in how they dress. Always managing to look at ease in their choices, they never let us forget that the real stars are the people wearing the clothes, not the outfits themselves.

IT'S NOT ABOUT MONEY, HONEY

Style is not about how much you spend but what you spend it on. A high school student can exhibit indisputable lady-style in her combination of thrift-store finds and inexpensive basics, while the wealthiest woman can have a wardrobe of designer wear that merely says "I can afford it."

Candice Bergen is a favorite of ours. Her sense of humor and attitude brings to her classical beauty a style that is elegant, understated, and ageless. Yet among her favorite clothes are tees and khakis. She eschews trends (she once remarked, "I'd rather be shot than wear a bustier"), wears only mascara and sheer lipstick, and makes her mark through distinctive accessories such as a favorite cuff bracelet.

Actress Julianna Margulies has always had great style, even when she was working as a waitress before getting her big break. Her favorite outfit is still the same one she wore through the lean years: Levis and a white T-shirt.

LETTING HER ASSETS SHINE

Every person has something wonderful to emphasize. We say highlight it and ignore the rest. A lady knows there's no point crying in her coffee about her wide hips, limp hair, modest bosom, or undefined waistline. She has the good sense to take the good with the bad, downplay

Superstar Style Doesn't Have to Be Expensive

It took a superstar like Sharon Stone to remind us that how good you look has nothing to do with wearing the latest fashion. At the 1996 Academy Awards—an event that is as much a fashion show as a film competition—Stone was the picture of confidence and elegance in a long black skirt and short-sleeved black turtleneck top. When asked who designed her outfit, Stone replied that she had waffled between a designer dress and this ensemble, a skirt by Valentino with the top from . . . the Gap. We rest our case.

the latter and play up her assets, and knows that no clothes in the world are as beautiful as the distinctive look she was born with.

If a lady has great legs, she knows how to highlight them. If she's blond and looks great in blue, she wears it as often as she can. If she's got Italian race-car curves like Sophia Loren, she shows them off! No one's perfect, but a lady knows looking great gives her the kind of confidence that only adds to her allure.

THE ART OF DRESSING APPROPRIATELY

Above all, a lady has good manners, which means she knows that certain times and places require certain modes of dress.

- A lady always heeds the dress code on an invitation. She knows the difference between black-tie and white-tie (for a woman, black-tie means formal dress, while white-tie means floor-length dress and nothing shorter), cocktail, and casual.
- She doesn't wear white to a wedding, or anything else that might detract from the bride.
- A lady wears black or dark, subdued colors to a funeral.
- She knows that jeans are appropriate only for casual events; ditto shorts; double-ditto workout wear, which is best reserved for, well, working out.
- Although it seems today that at many companies anything goes, a lady makes an effort to look pulled together so she is always taken seriously. Even on "casual Friday," which

usually means no suit required, she doesn't wear anything that lets her or others forget they're at work.

- Of course, there are businesses where a uniform, be it literal or figurative, is the most appropriate choice; a lady knows how to make even that reflect her personality.

- A lady doesn't dress in an overtly sexy way at the office or an interview, at school, family events, or religious ceremonies. Slinky clothes are appropriate for nightclubs, nonwork parties, intimate evenings, and the bedroom. Even then, the way she is dressed should invoke admiration, not ogling, resentment, or car wrecks. Subtlety is the key. As legendary Hollywood costume designer Edith Head once said, "A dress should be tight enough to show you're a woman, but loose enough to prove you're a lady."

- Given the choice, a lady would always rather be overdressed than underdressed for an occasion. She errs on the side of too much regard for her hosts, rather than too little.

BUILDING HER WARDROBE

Creating a wardrobe has nothing to do with the size of a lady's wallet and everything to do with the size of her brain. Open her closet and you will see clothes that have served her well for years, that reflect who she is, and that work together in different combinations. As with building a financial portfolio, she buys with an eye to the future and for growth—and allows for a little risk.

A lady figures out what basics work for her and adds to them: this may be separates that can be dressed up or down, or it may include a versatile suit that can take her from day into evening and looks different with a switch of accessories. A smart shopper, she never finds herself with nothing to wear in the face of a last-minute invite. She makes sure she has at least one appropriate ensemble in her closet for a dressy occasion, and a few choices for events such as a dinner party, a wedding, or a funeral.

Dini: "My grandmother handed down some wise advice to my mother who gave it to me: if, while you are shopping, you find something that is perfect for an evening affair, even if you don't have something specific to wear it to, buy it. This saves you in the future from last-minute spending on something you may not like as much and that may even cost more, and also saves you from the feeling that you have nothing to wear."

Press On

Brooke Astor has some plain wisdom for the art of style. "I think your clothes should be very clean and fresh and always in good shape," she said. "Go along that way, and you'll be all right."

THE FINISHING TOUCHES COUNT

A lady knows that the way she wears her hair, makeup, and accessories has as much to do with her style as the way she wears her clothes. Whether she chooses to keep it simple or changes her jewelry and hair on a regular basis, she knows these things finish off her look.

Hair. Not just her hairstyle but even its color creates an idea for other people about who she is. As Gwyneth Paltrow, whose roles sometimes require her to make major hair changes, said, "I do generally go for simple. But I've found that since my hair's been brown, I can get away with a lot more. When you're a blonde, that's a lot to take in, and I think you should be very tasteful and understated."

A lady does not torture herself over her hair. She finds a look, or several looks, she likes that flatter her and sticks with it (or them). If she enjoys constantly changing her hair and considers doing so part of her personal style, she doesn't let it become the foremost aspect of her appearance, but rather another accessory in her repertoire.

Let's Hear It for Versatility

Noelle: "My friend Sam has this silver floor-length skirt that she usually wears with sneakers and a T-shirt. Yet recently she wore it to attend a benefit dinner with a cashmere-and-sequin tank top, pearls, and heels! How's *that* for versatile?"

Dini: "I have a great gray suit that came with cropped pants and a skirt. I can't tell you how many times this suit has rescued me: I have worn it with high heels or, for a casual look, the pants with a sweater and flats; the jacket goes over different pants, and the skirt looks great with a long-sleeved top and high boots. This one suit gives me ten different looks, and they always work."

Makeup. With cosmetics, less is more, we say. (We've never heard anyone wish that a lady wore more of it!) A lady figures out what works best on her and sticks to it, establishing her own look.

Nails. Unless she's Flo-Jo and talons are her trademark, a lady's nails should not make others notice anything more than how well they are groomed. Our golden rule: never wear them so long you can't work on your computer or dial a phone. A lady doesn't aspire to the helpless look.

Jewelry. She might wear none at all (such as Carolyn Bessette Kennedy, who usually wore just her plain gold wedding band) or she may make her mark through individual pieces, but a lady never wears the contents of her jewelry box all at once. She also doesn't wear noisy jewelry, unless it's appropriate (such as in Morocco).

Perfume and scent. Smell is the strongest of the five senses. A lady always tries to smell good, whether she merely smells shower-fresh or puts a dab of perfume behind her ears and on her wrists. But she never overdoes it or wears an overpowering cologne. She picks one that goes well with her body scent, not just one that smells great on someone else.

PORTRAIT OF A LADY'S BASICS: A WORKING LIST

Some clothes are classics that exemplify style. They've withstood the tests of time and trends. They look as classic on a grandmother as they do on an eighteen-year-old. Whether they're paired with blue jeans, black leather, or they're dressed up, a lady knows the following pieces never fail:

- A well-cut white cotton button-down shirt
- A classic three-button navy or black jacket to toss over a business outfit, a dress, or even jeans
- A cardigan that looks equally great with jeans, dress pants, or a skirt
- A simple black dress that can be dressed down or up: always handy in a pinch
- A dress that looks nothing short of amazing on—for weddings, dinners, or any other dressy occasion (if she's really skilled, she'll find something that can be dressed down as well)
- A straight black skirt, to the knee or longer
- A pair of well-fitting jeans in a classic cut. A pair of black pants. A pair of dress slacks
- A pair of pearl or diamond studs (real or good fakes) so she's prepared for any formal or semiformal occasion
- A string of pearls (real or a good fake); they add simple elegance for day or evening
- A watch she can wear for both dressy and casual occasions
- Two good bags, one for day and one for evening

Quality over Quantity

A lady knows that it's better to spend a little more on quality items that she uses a lot than accumulate a slew of throwaway pieces that might not survive a year. Shoes and bras, for example, are items that she doesn't skimp on. They need to withstand lots of use and provide solid foundations and support so that we don't feel compelled to throw them into a blazing fire at the end of a long day. A good bag (be it a leather knapsack or a great purse) also lasts forever.

- A couple of pairs of flats in colors to match her wardrobe
- A pair of black boots
- A pair of black high heels (that she can walk in)
- One good coat; for example, a long black wool coat never goes out of style

A lady also knows that having her clothes fit well is part of looking sharp. Her tailor (or her sewing box) is her friend.

Most important of all, a lady knows there's no accessory like confidence. It can make someone in a cotton dress outshine a self-conscious slouch in the most expensive Armani gown.

STYLE TRADEMARKS

A lady knows that classic clothes don't have to look ordinary. With trademarks, a lady makes an outfit her own. It can be the way she always wears red lipstick, or a particular watch, or how she's known for cool shoes or a great hairstyle. A trademark may be a function of comfort and ease (Katharine Hepburn and her pants), a function of necessity (Jacqueline Kennedy Onassis and the big oval sunglasses she wore to hide from the paparazzi), a sentimental or favorite accessory, or the way she plays up her best asset.

Some stylish ladies' trademarks:

Carolyn Bessette Kennedy: a chignon, never wearing jewelry

Andie MacDowell: long curly hair, romantic clothes

Isabella Rossellini: short hair, white blouses, men's suits
Madeleine Albright: lapel pins, a Stetson
Brooke Astor: white gloves and hats
Whoopi Goldberg: dreadlocks, wide-legged pants

Many of our survey respondents had trademarks:

"A vintage watch for every day of the week"
"Hoop earrings, big curly hair!"
"Intelligent specs and a no-fuss bob"
"Navy blue—it's all I wear"
"Two small silver rings on my left thumb that I have not re-
    moved in years!"
"Ten pairs of cool running shoes that I wear with everything"

Actress Julianna Margulies shared her trademark with us:

*I always seem to find a way to incorporate a pair of trou-
sers into my outfit. I'm not a skirt or dress girl. I'm a pant
girl. I think it's because I was such a tomboy as a kid and
the idea that you can run much easier in a pair of pants
than a skirt always appealed to me. Also, in England we
had to wear skirts to school every day, so it's probably a
little bit of rebellion. The trick, however, now that I'm an
adult (how sad), is to make a great pair of pants look feminine and sexy.*

LADY STYLE ICONS: AUDREY, KATHARINE, AND JACKIE

Audrey Hepburn, Katharine Hepburn, and Jacqueline Kennedy Onassis were the women whose style our survey respondents most admired, with Audrey taking the number-one spot by far. (It's interesting to note that all three were early proponents of pants for comfort!) Audrey Hepburn's style truly reflected who she was: elegant, thoughtful, fun, classic, casual, and glamorous. Perhaps that's part of why another lady, Christy Turlington, said she viewed Audrey as the historical figure with whom she most identified. Our respondents weighed in on what they saw in Audrey:

- "Always classy, even when totally casual"
- "She was effortlessly perfect"
- "Not that her particular style is me, she was just the perfect lesson in what style is all about"
- "She is, to me, the epitome of grace and beauty and love and everything that's good in this world"

Audrey wore clothes that reflected her personality. While she could afford designer clothes and loved dressing up, she made her mark with minimal fuss—capris, sweaters, flats, and a pixie haircut. Her clothes were about being comfortable and free to move. As a result, the true Audrey—graceful and caring—shone through.

The other Hepburn, Katharine, was known for her iconoclastic style. She made pants look as feminine and elegant as dresses, which she assiduously avoided. "I like to move fast, and wearing high heels was tough, and low heels with a skirt is unattractive. So pants took over," she once said.

Few would argue the superlative style of Jacqueline Bouvier Kennedy Onassis. Her life in the public eye served as a stage on which she exemplified style in all its manifestations—from her clothes to her restoration and decorating of the White House to her understanding that, as a first lady with small children, she served as a role model for many American women. This had been ingrained in her by her father, who told her, "Style is not a function of how *rich* you are, or even *who* you are. Style is a habit of mind that puts quality before quantity, noble struggle before mere achievement, honor before opulence. It's *what* you are. It's your essential self."

What makes Audrey, Katharine, and Jackie style icons with staying power is that we always noticed them first, and then their clothes. Of course, their clothes were always great, but even more, they suited their wearers well. These ladies knew that looking sharp gave them confidence to succeed in whatever they did.

There are many ladies today whose great and greatly varying style may make them style icons tomorrow. Singer-rapper Lauryn Hill with her casual but high-style clothes and the feminine grace she brings to hip-hop; Uma Thurman in her urban-mother chic; Toni Morrison with her fabulous, flowing gray hair; Sarah McLachlan in her Indian tunics.

McLachlan defined her style: "When I stopped caring about what everybody else thought, I really came into my own style. My husband is East Indian, and in his culture they wear long tunics with pants underneath. I thought it looked really cool." Sometimes that's all the reason a lady needs.

THE BEST ACCESSORY IS CONFIDENCE

The most important ingredient in the recipe for lady-style is self-assuredness. Without components such as confidence, originality, verve, humor, or resourcefulness, a lady's style is nothing. All the beautiful clothes in the world will look like a burlap sack on a woman who is ill at ease with herself.

There is nothing so becoming as a woman with grace and a confident smile. An example stands out: the late Oseola McCarty lived a modest life of anonymity until several years ago, when she quietly announced that she was donating her life savings to a university so that young women can have the scholarship opportunities not available to her when she was young. In the photograph that accompanied her obituary, McCarty was the picture of style. She was wearing a plain but elegant tailored dress and some simple jewelry. One accessory stood out above all: a broad, proud smile.

HOME STYLE

I think people who come into my home feel comfortable
and welcome and loved. And the biggest thing in my
living room [the fireplace] is in and of itself an
expression of love. —JULIA ROBERTS

Like our clothes, our homes also give us the opportunity to be creative. At home we can cut loose more—after all, not as many people are laying eyes on our sofas as they are on our clothes. A lady's home decor reflects what's important to her in a way that pleases her eye and allows for comfort.

Home is the place where a lady lets her hair down, where she can be herself. If she's an avid reader, her living room walls may have floor-to-ceiling bookshelves; if she loves works of art—whether it's her child's crayon drawings, her framed Matisse poster, or her collection of black-and-white photographs—she'll hang them; if cooking's her thing, you can be sure she's paid special attention to her kitchen and dining room, and they'll be places you'll want to hang out.

Put Your Feet Up

"What's important to me in a house is that there's a tremendous sense of comfort. Every chair you sit in is comfortable. If you can't sit back, you're just in transit. If you're perched on a chair, you're perched to leave. Life is too short not to be comfortable." —CANDICE BERGEN

She creates a home that reflects her individuality and welcomes and comforts her friends and family.

A few things every lady knows about home style:

Less is more. Her home isn't overdone because she's confident in her choices. She picks her furnishings and decorations with care, knowing that one thoughtfully chosen piece can say more about a person than ten tchotchkes. It's also less distracting. A lady's aim is to create a welcoming home where everything works together and nothing stands out. Money is much less important to creating a stylish home than thought and care.

Lighting. Good lighting enhances a room. As Candice Bergen said: "I love lamps. Don't even talk to me about track lighting. I love lamps for the warmth they give a room, for the way the light comes through the shade."

Common scents. Scent makes a home feel alive. The smell of herbs, flowers in bloom, or candles burning provides warmth and puts people at ease. Jacqueline Kennedy always made it a point to have the fireplaces in the White House lit for warmth and aroma.

Neat and tidy. A lady tries to keep her home clutter-free and neat enough to readily welcome an unanticipated guest. While pets and children are a delight, a lady knows that they, and their stuff, have their place, which is not all over the house. For those who loathe cleaning, we reiterate Isabella Rossellini's good advice, passed down to her by her mother, Ingrid Bergman: "Never leave a room empty-handed."

A lady's style at home is original, reflecting her personality and her love for those with whom she shares it. We love what Julia Roberts did to make her home truly her own: she carved a favorite line of a Thomas Hardy poem into her wooden fireplace. It says, "Love is brave, sweet, prompt, precious as a jewel . . ."

FOUR

friendship: a lady delivers

*You have to work at your friendships with the same
seriousness you did when you went to school. You
studied for that, so you study for this.*
—TONI MORRISON

MARY ANN CROSS (better known as George Eliot, the pseudonym
she took to become a published writer in the Victorian era) described the condition of friendship as "having neither to weigh
thoughts nor measure words, but pouring them out just as they
are." It's true. Friends are like home. They're that place we can
come to relax, put up our feet, have some fun, and find relief from
the rest of the world. We know that with them we can cut loose,
be ourselves, and never worry about being judged.

Good friends support us in our time of need, keep our most
embarrassing secrets, listen patiently while we tell them the same
story over and over. They give us that needed kick in the pants
when no one else will; they tell us when we need to touch up our
roots; and they never, ever consider dating one of our exes.

Or, as Maria Shriver wrote, "Friends are people who reflect different aspects and interests of your life. . . . They help me with the kids, tell me I don't have to be Superwoman, warn me if I'm not being true to myself, and scream that I don't have to lose another five pounds. Girlfriends are the ones who fill in the gaps and pick up the slack left by your primary relationship. That's what friends are for."

Our modern lady understands the preciousness of friendship. For that reason, she doesn't take her friends for granted, she expects a great deal from them, and she delivers the same. When we asked our survey respondents what qualities they look for in a friend, here are some they cited:

Trustworthiness, open-mindedness, honesty, inspiration, loyalty, sense of humor about themselves, candor, intelligence, openheartedness, warmth, strength, sharing, good listening skills, self-respect, chutzpah, selflessness, commitment, independent thinking, authenticity, someone who is a friend despite long interims without speaking, flexibility, confidentiality, creativity, someone who will pick me up at the airport if I ask, a good advocate, outspokenness, healthy cynicism, tact, nuttiness, internal beauty, someone I don't need to impress.

(Incidentally, when we asked our survey respondents if they filled their own bill, 100 percent responded with an unequivocal "yes.")

It's one thing to expect a lot from your friends, and still another to deliver as much as you demand. That is precisely what sets ladies apart from the rest. Bringing loyalty, honesty, trust, appreciation, support, understanding, and empathy to her friendships, a lady rarely disappoints and often shines beyond expectation. Anyone who has the good fortune to be friends with one of our ladies will no doubt be elevated, enchanted, and inspired by her presence.

The Power of Friendship

In times of trouble there are seven women in the United States I can call at any hour and say "Now. Now. I need you now." And they will come. No questions. No objections. . . . Nothing, nothing would keep them from me and me from them.—MAYA ANGELOU

A lady knows that friends look to each other for encouragement in the face of new challenges, compassion in the wake of disappointment, guidance in the face of uncertainty, and praise in the wake of accomplishments. Being supportive is sometimes about just being there for a friend, being a good listener, refraining from offering advice or moralizing, or respecting a friend's point of view. Other

Ladies Appreciate Their Friends

Rebecca from New York City wrote to us about the special way she shows her friends how much they mean to her. We hope this story will inspire you as much as it did us:

I truly believe it takes a village to raise a child, and I believe that each interaction, each relationship, contributes to the person I am. So when my mom (my best friend, hero, and biggest cheerleader) is not around me, my best (girl)friends help "raise" me. All of these women had heard

→

79

about each other over the years (some live outside of NYC). One day I decided I wanted to gather all these amazing women together. So during Women's History Month, I hold a "Brunch in Your Honor"—a day where my gal-pals come and relax, eat, and feel divine. At the brunch, which has now become a tradition (six years and counting), I tell each of the women what their friendship means to me, and what qualities I love/respect/admire about them. . . . I believe that it's too late to eulogize someone when they are gone.

times it's about giving our friends a good-natured reality check, like the one Candice Bergen writes of in her autobiography, *Knock Wood:*

What made [turning thirty] easier [for me] were friends. My friends were my extended family: true-blue, old-shoe, longtime friends. . . . Friends with whom nothing sacred, no-holds-barred behavior prevailed. . . . It was my friends who gave me a sense of proportion about my attacks of Premature Mid-Life Crisis, and who steadily kidded me out of my coma. . . . I was devoted to them, indebted, and I wanted to be as available to them as they had been to me.

WHEN THE GOING GETS TOUGH

A lady is not a fair-weather friend. She is the rock others look to for support in a time of need. She is also there when a friend doesn't have the courage to ask for help. Many of our survey respondents offered anecdotes about friends who had been there in a time of need. They ran the gamut from hysterically funny to heart-wrenching. Here's just a sampling:

"My friend took my children away for a day without being asked, while my husband and I got some time with our newborn." —Dana, Brockton, MA

"When my goldfish died (he jumped out of the bowl), I couldn't bear to pick him up, so my friend Shawn came over and helped pick him up and flush him down the toilet! Now that's a real friend!" —Rebecca, New York City

"When I was in the throes of my separation from my husband and felt terribly uncomfortable sharing our small one-bedroom apartment in NYC, my friends Vanessa, Betsy, and Dana opened their homes and hearts to me on alternating nights for about three weeks until he finally moved out. They made me dinner, held me up, and acted as my cheerleaders through a heartbreaking period. I will never forget them for it." —Susannah, Southport, CT

"My friend Pam came with me to visit my parents at my grandfather's cabin while my mother was ill with ALS (Lou Gehrig's disease). By this point she needed help going to the toilet, which Pam did without batting an eye. Like it was no big deal." —Amy, Norwalk, CT

"I was raped as a teenager and as a result got pregnant. With the support (financially and emotionally) of my closest friend, I terminated the pregnancy and went through counseling. I am forever grateful. She allowed for me to regain my self-worth, and she never doubted me or my decision." —Anonymous

WHEN THE GOING GETS GOOD

*I just can't appreciate all [this success] unless the people
I care about are there having a good time with it.*

—SANDRA BULLOCK

To Lend or Not to Lend, That Is the Question . . .

Sometimes being supportive means helping a friend out of a difficult situation. Dana from Brockton, Massachusetts, learned how much that could mean when her relationship ended and her boyfriend took the furniture. She wrote, "My friend furnished my entire apartment . . . and told me to pay her back when I could."

Lending money has always been thought of as →

While a lady is there for her friends in times of trouble, she also lends support to those who experience success. To quote Oscar Wilde: "Anybody can sympathize with the sufferings of a friend, but it requires a very fine nature to sympathize with a friend's success."

It meant the world to survey respondent Candace in Australia that her friends gathered to celebrate the completion and publication of her first book: *"When [it] was published, a group of fifteen to twenty writer friends of mine got together and threw a dinner to celebrate. It was one of the most concrete expressions of support and friendship I'd ever had, and I was deeply moved."*

TELLING IT LIKE IT IS

A friend is someone who will tell me what I need to hear, not just what I want to hear.

—DANA, BROCKTON, MA

In order for any relationship to survive, the truth needs to be told. The *truth*, as it were, could be something as benign as "Sweetie, that bias cut is not right for you," or as brutal as "I think it's time you accept that it's over between you and Frank and move on." Honesty between friends breeds a sense of deep trust that can't be reached otherwise. And that trust is what makes a friendship more than mere acquaintance.

Sometimes the truth does hurt, but a lady knows that real friendship will survive conflict, and she does her best to express her feelings—no matter how controversial they might be. (After all, if she can't be honest with friends, what's the point?)

Of course, there are risks involved in broaching a subject a friend might not be ready to hear, so a lady thinks before she opens her mouth. For example, if a

taboo, and we've all been told at one time or another that the exchange of money between friends is a surefire relationship-killer. This is probably why 37 percent of our survey respondents, when asked if they'd lend money to a friend, wrote that it was a "bad idea." Interestingly, the other 63 percent said they would hand over the money to a friend in need without a second thought.

We say a lady knows how to handle situations in which she or a friend is in serious financial straits—without straining the relationship. A lady will help her friends in any way, provided she can afford to do so without putting her own finances in jeopardy. Conversely, she will not be afraid to ask for help if she really needs it. What's the point of having good

→

83

friends if you can't turn to them in times of need?

We believe the problems that arise from lending money have nothing to do with the loan itself, and everything to do with the payback. Which is why our final point is this: a lady makes repaying a debt her first priority. And out of respect for her helpful friend, she does not treat herself to frivolous or luxury purchases until she is fully in the black.

friend is wallowing in self-pity about a relationship that went awry, a lady will indulge her, be supportive, and say the predictable yet supportive clichés like "There are other fish in the sea . . . you deserve better." However, if the woeful friend did something to cause the demise of the relationship (cheated, was pathologically jealous), a lady won't candy-coat the truth. Rather, she may give her friend some advice to aid in future romantic endeavors. A lady knows her friendships can withstand the truth, no matter how unwelcome it might be on occasion. While she may feel compelled to comment, she always forgives her friends a temporary lapse in judgment.

Should a lady tell a friend if she knows his or her partner is straying? In our on-line survey, about 28 percent said, "No way!"—citing that they had done so in the past and lost a friend because of it. Another 69 percent responded, "Absolutely! Without a doubt! I'd expect my friends to tell me!"

Close friends have an awesome responsibility when they know something like this. While in the past, our mothers (and their mothers) were probably advised to keep quiet and keep out of it, times have changed, and our kind of lady would never betray a good friend with silence. Nor would she act impulsively, or without giving the situation a great deal of thought.

Before telling someone outright, a lady might try to find out whether her friend *wants* to know—based on whether he or she has said anything that indicates suspicion, or expressed particular feelings about infidelity in the past. It's important to recognize that sometimes people *don't* want to know, because then they don't have to deal with it. As always, a lady gauges the situation before she moves forward. (Ladies—this might be a good time to call your friends and ask how they'd like you to handle a similar situation. We did!)

Suffice to say, a lady is honest with only one intention: to do right by her friend. Whether she's telling her friend his "famous" turkey chili should be retired forever; to rethink meeting a chatroom Romeo in person; or that her partner might be straying, she does it without relish and with genuine concern for her friend's happiness and well-being.

HER FRIENDS AND LOVERS

Never make your friends feel like replacements for when your guy isn't around. Find time for a girls' night out, no matter what's going on in your life.

—SHOSHANNA LONSTEIN

When a lady enters into hot-and-heavy romance, she knows to resist the temptation to build her own little solar system around herself and her new partner. Sure, we're human, and in the throes of new love, sometimes we get carried away. But not for long, because a lady never forgets her friends and how important it is to stay in touch. When she finds that perfect partner, the last thing she'd want to do is stop being a good friend.

Most people understand when their friends fall off the face of the earth in the beginning of a relationship. In fact, the smitten one is probably doing them a favor. Few things are more tiresome than trying to have a conversation with some mooning, sighing pal who can only talk about her sweetie-pie, love muffin, [insert other pet name here] . . .

But once the smoke, glitter, and clouds clear, a lady comes to her senses and remembers that her friends are her foundation and support system—not just for when the going gets tough, but also for when the going gets great! If she stops calling her friends, stops making plans to see them, or worse, feels justified in canceling plans when The One calls at the last minute, a lady is committing a friendship felony.

Bottom line? A lady spares her friends as much gushing blabber as she can, remembers they have lives and needs, too, and never gives friends the backseat to a lover for long. She'd hate to risk losing them for good.

FRIENDSHIP TAKES EFFORT

A lady values her friends immensely. For this reason, she makes every effort to sustain friendships, despite thousands of miles and/or a busy life. This can be as simple as keeping regular contact or as sublime as an unexpected gesture of appreciation.

A lady never lets a friendship shrivel on the vine if it is important to her. It can be hard to make time in a busy day, and busy life, to keep up with our friends, but we don't need hours to spare to maintain a friendship. Even busy leading lady Sandra Bullock finds time with her drum-tight posse in Austin, Texas, to throw barbecues and club crawls—and they've even formed their own traveling book club to facilitate get-togethers as often as possible.

It's important to a lady that she keep constant contact and check in with her friends, whether she does it via e-mail, letters, phone calls, or sending a thoughtful gift simply because it made her think of her friend. Alex in Rochester, New York, wrote, "My friend Naomi is incredibly thoughtful. If I mention something I've seen and loved, six months later it'll arrive as a present for my birthday or a holiday. She remembers the littlest things in a way that I can only aspire to."

A Lady "Just Says No" to a Friend's Ex

Ninety-nine-point-nine percent of our survey respondents said a friend's ex is absolutely out of the question as a potential mate—unless, by some act of the gods, he or she is her "soul mate." A lady knows there are plenty of baggage-free people out there without having to settle for a friend's unwanted (or worse, still desired) leftovers. Dating or hooking up with a friend's ex is in bad taste, disloyal, suspect in its motivations, and last but not least, hardly ever worth it.

THE AUTHORS' TURN TO GUSH

Since we have been friends for nearly fifteen years, we thought we'd give our readers some insight into the depth of our friendship, what it means to each of us, and how we've managed to survive the challenges many friendships face.

Noelle: Dini and I met while we were both working campus security during our freshman year of college (no doubt subsidizing our bar tab at the Mug, the on-campus nightclub). She was the city girl all the guys wanted to date, the sophisticated, cosmopolitan fashion plate who lent an air of mystery and intrigue wherever she went. I was a naïve fish out of water, coming from a small blue-collar town in Connecticut and experiencing my first months away from home. In spite of our different backgrounds, we became fast friends and have been ever since. (Perhaps academia is the great equalizer after all. . . .)

We've survived crushes on the same guy, competing for acceptance into a highly competitive writing program (one of us made it), and yes, writing a book together about what it means to be a lady in the new millennium. Over the last fourteen years, Dini has been there for me through several tough breakups (even a marriage gone sour), the loss of my father to cancer, and countless other day-to-day dramas. She also has been one of my most dogged cheerleaders and has, on more than one occasion, given me the kick in the pants I needed when no one else was brave enough. While we certainly have differences of opinion on many subjects, we respect each other's outlooks. And although we live on opposite sides of the country, we are sure to check in on each other as often as our hectic schedules permit. I've had the pleasure of watching Dini become the kind of mother I can only hope to become one day, and as I watch her daughter, Tati, grow up, I know in my heart she is on her way to becoming the kind of lady who will make her mother very proud.

Dini: When I met Noelle, I thought she was the exact opposite of me: tall, blond, striking, hip, looking like she knew exactly what she was doing. I wanted to know her better. (I was hoping that some, if not all, of her cool traits would rub off on me.)

It wasn't until becoming close with Noelle that I understood a true friendship can survive any trial. We have gone through so much in our last fifteen years and are all the closer for it.

In the beginning of this chapter, when we described the qualities our survey respondents said they looked for in friends, it was I who had written, "Will pick me up at the airport." Of course it's metaphorical, but Noelle was the first person who ever picked me up from the airport in a major city where getting a cab was no problem. Silly as it sounds, I found that astounding and immensely generous. (We New Yorkers never pick anyone up at the airport!)

That's Noelle. Unfailingly generous, funnier than she will ever know, smart, sharp, wise, giving, humble, stylish, kooky, a great dancer. Ultra-cool.

What I love most about Noelle is the clarity with which she sees so many situations. I can go on and on about something, and in a few words, she can sum up and define it. Through heartache and joy, laughter and tears, and many cups of tea (Noelle) and coffee (me), we have grown together.

They say blood is thicker than water, but what runs through her veins runs through mine. I think not of what we would do for each other if necessary but of what we wouldn't. Nothing.

FIVE

in the workplace: ladies set the standard

There were rules of the road for men and women in social settings, but we were improvising a new etiquette in the office as we moved along. These were days of great confusion for everyone. . . . Everyone was touchy about the rights and wrongs, even if we didn't know exactly what they were.
—LESLEY STAHL

WOMEN HAVE made incredible strides in the last thirty years. Today there are more of us in the workforce, in upper management, and running businesses than ever before. Not only do we make up 50 percent of the workforce, but 51 percent of mothers work outside the home. While we've fought long and hard to carve out a place for ourselves in the traditionally male workplace, our struggles certainly didn't end with "Congratulations, you're hired." Once we got the jobs, we, just like men, had to learn how to handle different personalities, power struggles, team dynamics, hierarchy, competition, physical attraction on the job, and much more. Add to that the daunting task of learning and understanding the rules of the workplace, rules that were invented and mastered by men long before women had even one foot in the door. A tall order, to say the least.

For most people, work is a means to an end, the way we pay our bills. For others, it is how we define ourselves and achieve personal fulfillment. Between the two of us, we've been working for thirty-four years. In that time we've seen nearly every variety of work style, communication style, and work environment—from the newsroom to the corporate conglomerate, from the mom-and-pop business to the nonprofit organization. From the good to the bad to the ugly.

While women have been told that they have to act more like men to get ahead, we say that a lady is the true star of the workplace—whether she is a CEO, firefighter, waitress, or sales clerk.

A positive work experience has less to do with the makeup of the office than it does with the attitude of the people working in it. Recognizing this, a lady does her part to create a positive work culture by bringing her indisputable grace and dignity, as well as a generous helping of patience, consideration, and humor, to the table.

Our culture does not reward consideration and respect for others. In fact, some might be foolish enough to say that these attributes impede professional success. But a lady knows that short-term maneuvering and attention seeking never last as long as durable relationships and great work accomplished over time.

SIX LADY MAXIMS FOR THE WORKPLACE

- Good manners are good manners—no matter where you are.
- Work is not a social occasion, and maintaining professional boundaries is essential.
- There's no room for oversize egos at work.
- Just as sports, the workplace needs teamwork to thrive.
- Have the self-respect to know and go after what you're worth and the good sense to know when to move on . . . gracefully.
- It's not required that you like everyone you work with, but it's essential that those you don't care for never know it.

A lady has a strong work ethic, is confident in her capabilities, and is prepared to deal with the challenges of her job. She's a team player who doesn't put her own advancement over the organization's betterment, and she knows that above and beyond doing her job well, there are certain courtesies in the workplace that enhance *everyone's* work experience. No, she's not perfect.

No one is. But as we all know, a lady works hard to keep the standards high wherever she goes.

GOOD MANNERS AND OTHER BASICS

A lady always treats her colleagues with the same courtesy and respect that she expects for herself.

She respects other people's time by being punctual to appointments, informing the people expecting her rather than apologizing afterward if she's going to be late, and returning phone calls and answering inquiries promptly.

She refrains from vulgar language at the office—no matter how angry she may be, no matter how much her boss or colleagues swear. Why? Because profanity is unprofessional and usually unnecessary to get a point across.

She keeps her work space neat because sloppiness implies carelessness (not a good impression) and it's discourteous to her coworkers, even if she has her own door to close. Furthermore, a lady knows that the workplace is where she does her job, and while her office may reflect her personality, it is not the place to make political statements, show religious affinities, or display art or photographs that might create unwanted distractions or make others uncomfortable. (So, no matter how "hot" her boyfriend looks without his shirt on, she saves those sexier shots for her bedside table.)

She doesn't get seduced by office gossip. As innocuous as it may seem in the moment, idle chatter about coworkers can cause unforeseen damage. An offhand comment about seeing your boss with the VP of sales over the weekend could have serious repercussions. Frankly, it's no one's business. If you're willing to talk about others, you may be seen as untrustworthy or, worse, become a fair target yourself. Remember our rule: when in doubt, ask yourself—is it true? Is it kind? Is it necessary? If not, a lady thinks twice.

She tries to maintain a positive attitude at work (even if others try to bring her down). A lady knows that negativity is counterproductive and that someone who is unhappy, cynical, uncooperative, or elitist creates a barrier to getting the job done. Her positive attitude is infectious, and as the saying goes, the rising tide lifts all ships. Sure, everyone has bad days. But even a bad day doesn't excuse a spur-of-the-moment tantrum or an unbridled outburst of frustration—however justified it might feel in the heat of the moment.

She's not a blabbermouth. A lady doesn't share confidential information about any aspect of her company with anyone. No matter how friendly she is with her colleagues outside of work, she doesn't talk with them about salaries, career plans, or such inside information as impending layoffs. Confidential information is given to her based on trust, and while spilling the beans may seem tempting, it makes her look gossipy and maybe unethical.

She knows technophobia is no excuse. A lady makes sure she knows how to operate her phone, her computer, the copier, the fax machine, and any other piece of equipment that is integral to the performance of her job. She'd be embarrassed to stand by vacantly while someone else deals with it. And for the record, *no one is above refilling the paper tray!*

She knows the difference between social and professional functions. A lady understands that an office event is not the place to showcase a clingy dress with a plunging neckline, rehash old college glories by drinking the tech department under the table, or put the moves on "that cute guy in sales." (Really, everyone should know this by now—but you'd be surprised.) She understands that even though music is playing, food and alcohol are being served, and people are laughing, the office party is still a business function. As mind-numbing as some business functions can be, a lady always drinks in moderation so as not to become Monday's watercooler topic, or worse, the evening's unscheduled entertainment.

She dresses appropriately. Although offices vary in the degree of formality observed, a lady takes her cues from her immediate superior's attire, as well as from coworkers she respects. She need not suppress her individuality, but she knows the difference between clothes, hairstyles, and accessories that are appropriate and those that might distract or make others uncomfortable. As we've intimated before, the workplace is not a singles bar or a fashion show. So no matter how great you look in that snake-print skirt or fishnets, save those pieces for nights out. (For more on this, see the Style chapter.)

Listen Up

In meetings, unless she is running them, a lady listens to everyone else's point of view before speaking her mind. Not only will her opinion be better informed, but she will also get people used to looking forward to hearing what she has to say.

—JADA, CONCORD, NH

THE TIME AND THE PLACE

A lady knows implicitly that the workplace is not a social setting. She also knows that work colleagues are not her intimates, but fellow members of a team. She may have little more in common with them than the signature on their paychecks, so a lady always maintains professional boundaries.

She doesn't share too much personal information, or ask others to; she knows liking and being liked are secondary to getting the job done; she knows how to laugh but would never make her coworkers uncomfortable; most of all, she expects the same of others and lets them know it. She does her part to keep them all focused on *working* together.

THE RISKS OF OFFICE ROMANCE

Sure, it happens. Your eyes meet while you're both waiting for the fax machine . . . you have lunch or cappuccino a couple of

When Boundaries Blur . . .

When I was the creative director at a small ad agency, I became good friends with a woman I hired as a writer. Soon, though, I found that we were spending more time in my office talking about non-work-related topics (our gardens, our dogs, our husbands' similar quirks . . .) than doing our jobs. I realized that I had to put some distance between us for the

→

sake of my team. The last thing I wanted people to think was that I was favoring one person over another because I had more in common with him or her outside of work. I discussed my concerns with her and fortunately she understood my quandary. And even though I've since left the company and moved across the country, she and I are still fast friends.

—LILLY, TUCSON, AZ

Survey Says . . .

Forty-nine percent of ladies surveyed thought that it was all right to date someone they work with under the proper circumstances. Twenty-nine percent thought it was always a bad idea.

times a week . . . then he walks you to your car and asks to see you on the weekend. Because we spend the better part of our waking hours with the same people day in and day out, it's no wonder sometimes sparks fly between coworkers. But a lady knows that getting sexually and emotionally entwined with a colleague might disturb the balance at work—not just for the couple but for those around them. In those instances when an attraction is true destiny, a lady talks with her paramour about the possible consequences and ways to handle the situation. And she keeps the affair under wraps until it is a committed, stable relationship (to spare coworkers any confusion or discomfort). If there's even a whiff of conflict of interest, by the time the happy couple "goes public," one person should be taking measures to move to another department or out of the company altogether.

GO, TEAM, GO!

Above all, a lady knows that getting her job done requires everyone's cooperation.

She does not operate as a maverick in a team environment, and she can walk the fine line between excelling and being part of a group effort. She lets her boss lead and knows how to take direction. She also knows that on occasion she has to do things that aren't in her job description for the good of the team. As every lady knows, no one, not even an executive, is above making coffee or running an errand once in a while.

THE BOSS-LADY

When a lady is the boss, she takes her leadership position very seriously and brings her self-confidence, compassion, and patience to every situation. She recognizes that in most cases, she cannot be friends with her subordinates in the same way they can be with one another. She does not run the risk of undermining her own authority by not maintaining a proper distance.

> ### Creative Management
>
> Noelle: "A few years back, at a particularly low point for me personally, I was having an especially sad morning in my office. My boss, Roxanne, called me into her office, gave me ten dollars and sent me to a nearby bookstore, saying 'Go get some magazines, have a cup of tea, and come back when you're feeling better.' I will never forget her patience and understanding . . . not to mention her ability to calm me down and inspire me to work. She was savvy *and* sensitive enough to fix the potential problem in one benevolent gesture. A real lady."

She also remembers she's accountable for the work of her staff—especially when things go wrong. When those occasions arise, she is a buffer between her superiors and her subordinates,

No Lady Is an Island

When we asked *60 Minutes* coeditor and CBS news correspondent Lesley Stahl for her thoughts on ladies and the workplace, she immediately responded that loyalty was very important to her. "It's like King Arthur and the Round Table. We possess all these virtues of the knight, formerly perceived as manly—like loyalty and honesty. And now these virtues apply to women in the world of many different round-tables. I think female loyalty is essential to our success in the workplace."

and takes the heat rather than pointing a finger at a member of her staff.

Rewarding a job well done. A lady understands that the accolades she ascribes to a colleague or subordinate do not detract from her own value, and she always says thank you for a job well done. While it may seem obvious, in hectic organizations, the simple gesture of acknowledging someone's efforts is often overlooked.

Dini: "A member of my staff at the nonprofit AIDS education foundation Love Heals had put in a huge amount of overtime to get a really important (and *very* stressful) fund-raiser off the ground. I knew that she was contemplating taking up yoga but was unsure whether she'd like it. So I bought her a ten-class introductory series to thank her for all her hard work, and she fell in love with it."

In addition to the reward she gets for making someone's day, a lady knows that by recognizing others for their accomplishments, she inspires loyalty and respect from her team.

Managing "outside the box." A lady understands that being a good manager is about more than just getting the job done. She knows that her employees are not just cogs in a wheel but human beings. She does the unexpected, such as occasionally taking her staff out for lunch on her own dime, or giving comp days (if she can) to employees who go above and beyond or put in extra time.

A lady is a mentor. A lady wants her employees to learn from her experience, advance professionally under her tutelage, and look forward to coming to work every day. She knows that a fulfilled employee is a productive employee. She gives regular feedback to everyone, makes sure performance appraisals are done in a timely fashion, and makes herself available to answer questions or give advice about problems or issues that might arise.

She's not above getting her hands dirty in the trenches. Just because she's the boss doesn't mean a lady isn't part of the team. It is still her job to act as a role model for her subordinates. Marcia Kilgore, founder of

Conflict: Written vs. Verbal

In the age of e-mail, it has become all too simple to hide behind a keyboard during a heated argument (especially when your adversary is on another floor or just plain scary). Sure, e-mail eliminates sudden outbursts and raised voices, but quite often, disagreements escalate more rapidly and unnecessarily when conducted in writing.

A lady knows that by meeting face-to-face, she lessens the opportunities for misinterpretation. It also shows that she is open to the give-and-take of con-

→

101

versation, even if it's just a couple of minutes long. Many a working relationship has been unnecessarily strained by the time-consuming process of deliberately worded memos or, worse, those that are hastily read and misinterpreted. We've learned the hard way that even things as seemingly insignificant as all caps (most people read it as yelling and don't appreciate it), a comma in the wrong place, or too many exclamation points can cause hard feelings. The office is no place for hard feelings. One last thing: a lady never cc's (via e-mail or memo) other people without the explicit knowledge and, ideally, permission of the person with whom she is having this difference of opinion.

the highly successful Bliss Spa in New York City, sets a great example for ladies. Even though she's the company's CEO, Kilgore still does occasional facials, works fifteen-hour days, and answers the telephones in the booking office—even after selling her company for $30 million.

She *never* forgets the uphill struggle for women. A lady is sensitive to the unique challenges that women face in primarily male-dominated industries. If she is in a position of influence, she does what she can to help her fellow ladies.

CONFLICT RESOLUTION, LADY-STYLE

Eventually we are all faced with people with whom we disagree on many levels—from communication style to how to handle key company projects. While a lady is certainly not going to roll over when someone else transgresses, she does not let conflict fluster her. She has the self-esteem and confidence to face it head-on, in a manner that is graceful, dignified, and self-possessed. Sure, we all lose our cool once in awhile, but the important thing is to recognize when the heat gets unbearable and deal with it. The art of conflict resolution is something a lady aspires to master every day.

A lady knows when to stand her ground and when to agree to disagree. When she must argue, she sticks to the merits of the argument and doesn't let conflicts degenerate into personal attacks. When others are fighting, a lady looks to find resolutions. Rather than letting ill feelings fester, she knows the value of quickly dealing with and resolving conflicts.

Speak, don't yell. When she's been pushed to her limit, a lady will take a deep breath, think about what she wants to say, and say it in a controlled manner. She displays self-possession rather than lack of control. Even when she raises her voice, a lady doesn't scream. As we always say, "The louder you get, the more wrong you sound."

Handling someone who crosses the line. Likewise, when a lady is faced with a colleague who can't control his or her temper and begins to yell or speak in a disrespectful manner, she doesn't take it lying down. The best way we've found to handle such behavior is to say, in a very calm voice, "Please don't speak to me that way. I'd be happy to continue this conversation when you've calmed down a bit."

Say Something!

Ninety-four percent of ladies surveyed said they would address an offensive remark immediately by taking the offender aside, rather than ignoring it or saying something in front of other people.

103

Speaking Up Pays Off

Noelle: "When I was publishing director of a large computer company, I worked for a CEO (we'll call him Charles) who tested all of my training in diplomacy.

"One afternoon at a bimonthly meeting, Charles decided to go on one of his regular (and often amusing) tangents. He buzzed his secretary and asked her to bring in the first issue of a new men's magazine I'll call *Piston.* A colleague of his in London had just launched it with incredible success, and he wanted to share its "publishing genius." For what felt like an eternity, I sat between the two most powerful men in the company while one of them (Charles) flipped through each page of the premier

→

If that doesn't supplant the hysterics with embarrassment, we give up!

WHEN BOUNDARIES AREN'T ENOUGH

A lady knows that effective boundaries will often spare her behavior or language that would make her uncomfortable. However, some people are more obtuse than others. A lady knows when to choose her battles—when the potential gain is outweighed by the risks and/or impermeability of the offender's thick skull. Sometime her best defense might be to just ignore the comments and remove herself from the conversation. But if that isn't an option, a lady might take the offender aside and tell him/her calmly and nicely that what he/she said offended her (or others). A lady knows better than to say "What you said is offensive," because it puts the offender on the defensive; and what one person finds offensive, someone else might find innocuous or even entertaining. The most important point to get across is that she is not one of those who was entertained. Speaking her mind contributes to a work environment where others feel comfortable expressing themselves—which is always a good thing.

When a superior makes a move. Sometimes people forget the professional boundaries of the workplace and let their attractions get the better of their senses. When a lady is faced with an amorous superior, she is placed in a very precarious situation, one to be handled responsibly and delicately. We asked our survey respondents what they would do if faced with a boss who expressed romantic interest, and we wholeheartedly agree with the 96 percent who said they would politely decline and express their desire to maintain a professional-only relationship. Many also wrote that they would keep documentation of any inappropriate or persistent behavior and, if it got uncomfortable, would take up the issue with human resources. As flattering as they may appear, such incidents have often caused the demise of a woman's career.

issue of *Piston* UK—mostly seminaked women and articles about 'pulling birds.' As he put it, it was a 'manual for how to be a male chauvinist pig.'

"What I did next still shocks me to this day: I closed my binder, slid my seat back, said "Excuse me," and moved to the other end of the conference table. As the room grew silent, I turned the color of a cooked lobster. Just as suddenly, Charles closed the magazine and suggested that we resume the meeting.

"The meeting went on for another hour, and at its close, much unlike usual, everyone rushed to leave. As I collected my papers, Charles reentered the conference room and shut the door behind him. My palms began sweating and my mouth went dry. For the next sixty sec-

$\rightarrow$

onds, the CEO apologized for his rudeness and for making me uncomfortable in the meeting. He acknowledged that he was 'out of line' and said it would not happen again. I opened my mouth to say something like 'No big deal,' but only a breathy squeak came out as he opened the door and retreated to his executive office.

"In retrospect, I was rewarded in the best way I can imagine: thereafter I was treated with a new respect by Charles as well as the rest of my colleagues. (Sure, I was subjected to my fair share of feminist jokes once the dust settled, but that was a small price to pay to be spared any more *Piston* 'retrospectives.')"

SHE KNOWS WHAT SHE'S WORTH

A lady is not shy about her capabilities. She knows that the person interviewing her is looking for someone who has the skills for the position and may even be trying to compensate for a weakness in the organization. When a lady shows confidence in her own value, she is letting the interviewer know that she can do the job that needs to be done.

Traditionally, one of women's biggest weaknesses in business has been not asking for the salaries or bonuses that they deserve. (This explains why 12 percent of our survey respondents replied "I don't know" to the question "How do you get a raise?") A lady knows that a raise is about performance, what others in her profession get paid for similar work, and her commitment to the organization. As long as she delivers, she deserves recognition and appropriate compensation.

Furthermore, a lady is prepared to leave if she feels she isn't getting paid what she's worth. She knows that in most cases, making a leap to another organization is the best way to advance in her career, if that is her goal.

Time to move on. If and when a lady is dissatisfied with her job, she does everything within her power to change the situation. She talks to her supervisor, human resources, or union reps, and tries to make it work or get what she needs and deserves. If she is not satisfied with the outcome of her efforts, she moves on. A lady never lets her unhappiness at work percolate to the point that she spends more time scheming plots to undo her employer than actually taking steps to a more satisfying job. A lady understands that she is actually doing her company a favor by orchestrating a graceful exit and giving her boss a chance to find someone who can do her job with the enthusiasm she once had.

While it may at first feel calculated or, worse, uptight to abide by some of the ideas we've outlined above, it is important to remember that first and foremost,

Leaving Gracefully

We can think of no more ladylike a departure from a job than that of Jane Pauley from NBC's *Today* show in 1989. Thinking that the show needed a more youthful edge, NBC executives brought the younger, blonder news reader Deborah Norville on board, placing her side by side with cohosts Pauley, then thirty-eight, and Bryant Gumbel. Pauley was no fool, and although she had two years left on her contract, she resigned. On the morning of September 29, 1989, Pauley went on camera to thank NBC for "giving me this incredible front-row seat for the last thirteen years" and her colleagues "for being more like family." She then

→

graciously gave Norville the alarm clock that she had used to get up each morning for the show. Pauley's ladylike exit did not go unrewarded: shortly thereafter, she returned to the NBC fold as the evening cohost of its top-rated prime time show, *Dateline*, after management realized that she was who the people wanted.

the office is a place of work. This is not to say a lady stifles her enjoyment of her job or doesn't have fun. *Au contraire!* Her senses of humor and fun are critical to her sanity in a work environment—the place we spend most of our time, and over which we have the least input. Combine her dogged work ethic and interpersonal savvy with her positive and professional demeanor, and you have someone who will always be a valued part of any organization.

SIX

entertaining: a lady is
a hostess with the mostest

*Party giving is loving. It is giving. It is sharing. It is
everybody's chance to light a little candle in the
sometimes gloomy corners of the world.*
—ELSA MAXWELL

A PARTY thrown by a lady is always a hot ticket. When she's the
hostess, her guests know they're going to have a good time because her parties are fun and different and because she never
goes halfway. She succeeds because she thinks about her guests
above all and is never so caught up in trying to impress that they
don't enjoy themselves.

The secret to a lady's success is both creative and practical.
She makes it look easy, but whether they're poolside barbecues
or black-tie dinner-dances, her parties are well thought through.

The event will always be interesting because she'd rather cancel an event than bore her company.

A lady makes each of her guests feel important. She knows that just because she sets a beautiful table, offers the best champagne, or provides entertainment, this alone doesn't make for a good time. It's the way she melds the details that matters—a good mix of people and a festive mood, not to mention good eats. This is what makes her get-togethers far more than just the usual collection of familiar faces and a hot meal.

A LADY NEVER SWEATS THE SMALL STUFF

A lady knows that nothing kills the mood faster than if her guests feel like she's putting herself out at their expense, so she prepares in advance. There's nothing worse than a hostess who spends the first hour of her own party perspiring and clanging in the kitchen, ignoring her guests while they hope and pray she'll come out alive and unscathed. (We say that if throwing the shindig is going to take even a minute off your life, order takeout, hire a caterer, or reconsider.)

Still, even a lady can lose her grasp on the preparty preparations. She doesn't panic, she goes to Plan B. Either she'll arrange for help or ask a friend to assist or she'll change an aspect of the get-together so she's not overtaxed. Whether the event is a luncheon planned months in advance or an impromptu supper serving leftovers, a lady knows that becoming frazzled accomplishes nothing except making her guests feel like they'd rather be home.

Party Mix

*Never give a party if you will be the most interesting
person there.*—Mickey Friedman, mystery writer

A lady knows that people go to parties to escape the routine of everyday life. The last thing most people want to do at a party is see all the same folks they work with, bump into at school, or worship with under the same roof. A lady thinks about her guest list. She selects a variety of friends with different interests and careers so people can make new friends.

A lady is thoughtful enough to invite people with shared interests whose paths may not have crossed, or people who might hit it off romantically without feeling like they're being set up. Her parties are sure to have guests with a good sense of humor, because she values laughter and having fun. As a result of her efforts, a lady's guests go home enlivened from the stimulating time she gave them.

Screen legend Carole Lombard, who was well known for her love of a good time, once said, "Anyone who can afford to buy the booze can give a party, but it doesn't guarantee fun." At the actress's home, guests rubbed elbows with everyone from movie stars to sound technicians to studio heads to makeup artists.

A good hostess also makes sure to introduce her guests to one another, sharing a little bit about each or noting common interests so that they have a starting-off point for conversation.

She looks out for the shy guest who may be quietly keeping company with a lamp and finds a way to include him or her, perhaps asking for help in the kitchen or with the bar (which inevitably results in an exchange with others at the party).

A few tips:

- Never invite everyone you know, but select a diverse group. Gracefully break up cliques ("Excuse me, Judy, have you met . . .") so people mingle.
- With couples who have broken up, invite one or the other or discuss the issue with both. Don't ignore the potential for awkwardness (or drink throwing).
- If it's a small group, select your guests with care, particularly when some might have strong opposing political views (one way to handle this is to have a "no talk of politics" rule).

COMMUNICATION IS KEY

A lady is a good communicator. She isn't nebulous about details when she's organizing. If she's dead set on serving dinner at eight because she's timed the soufflés just so, she'll let her guests know to be prompt. She knows that in communicating everything from dress code to the party's occasion or theme, she's considering her guests' feelings. No one likes to show up inappropriately attired or too fashionably late, or in any other way to feel out of place.

In these days of four different types of vegetarians and countless trendy diets, it's nearly impossible to please all of the people all of the time. A lady shows the courtesy to ask her guests if they have dietary restrictions so she may offer options to satisfy everyone. After all, if they were important enough to invite in the first place, they're important enough to ask a simple question. Something as simple as a pasta or fish option can go a long way to making someone feel at home—and that's exactly her point.

If a guest calls to ask what he or she might bring to the party, a lady answers honestly. She either declines politely or suggests something specific that would add to the meal, such as a bottle of Chianti or a pint of chocolate ice cream, and thanks her guest for the offer. A lady's forthrightness will be appreciated, either way.

When a guest wants to bring a friend, a good hostess decides whether it's appropriate for the kind of party she's giving. (Dini: "Once, a friend of mine asked if he might bring a friend to a casual get-together I was having. I said yes, but then I thought to ask who it was. He turned out to be the lawyer representing the ex of a divorcing friend who was also coming! Crisis averted.") If it's an intimate birthday or anniversary party with just close friends or family, she may suggest that while she would always love to meet her friend's friend, another time would be better. But if the party's parameters are loose, then generally speaking, "the more the merrier" is a lady's attitude.

FOOD, GLORIOUS FOOD

The food at a lady's party is quite often the main attraction. Even if it may not be the center of the evening, bad food nearly always guarantees a flop, while a happy stomach makes a happy guest. For this reason, a lady puts thought into her menu. A lady need not be a gourmet chef or wine connoisseur to please the crowd.

Good food doesn't have to be fancy. Whether it's homemade fried chicken or roasted duckling, what matters is that the hostess has put her heart and soul into it and that her guests think it's delicious (nobody wants to have to fake compliments). Sometimes good old-fashioned soul food succeeds best of all: A-list Hollywood actress Sandra Bullock's two surefire recipes are her famous lasagna and "an apple crisp that brings the house down."

A lady knows her culinary limitations. A party is not the time to test a new recipe. If she does experiment, she informs her guests, who should be close friends. (And she has a backup pizza in the oven.)

Noelle: "I once invited six people over for homemade gnocchi. Not realizing that the ratio of semolina to potatoes was absolutely crucial, I was mortified when my gnocchi, once they hit the water, became potato soup. Thank heavens I had some dry pasta in my pantry so my guests could at least enjoy my homemade Bolognese sauce, which, if I may say so, is always a show stopper!"

If cooking's not her strong suit, a lady serves takeout or has someone else cook. There's no reason she can't throw a great party if the food comes from a favorite restaurant. This is a much better solution than turning herself inside out to manage a gourmet recipe that might turn out only half as tasty.

"I can't eat another bite; I'm stuffed!" are words every lady wants to hear. It means she's taken care of her grateful guests and done her job well.

Some tried-and-true tips we've collected:

- Have something to eat on hand from the moment your guests arrive. There's nothing worse than guests drinking on an empty stomach. Of course, hors d'oeuvres should not be so abundant that they cause guests to forgo the main course.
- Prepare at least enough food for seconds; guests should never go home hungry.
- When ordering takeout or using a caterer, make sure it's a restaurant or service you know and love.
- Two musts at any meal: bread and dessert. Bread is for the inevitable picky eater and dessert is for everyone. A lady knows that no matter how people protest about waistlines and diets, nothing caps off a good meal like dessert— whether it's something as simple as berries and cookies, as lavish as crème brûlée, or as homespun as hot apple pie à la mode.
- If she's serving wine with dinner, she makes sure it's one that will complement the meal.

- If she has a signature dish that her friends love, she serves it often.
- When in doubt, simple is better.

Cocktails and Mocktails

An easy way a lady can be creative is with what she serves to drink. She knows guests appreciate being offered an alternative to the age-old query "Red or white?" Whether the occasion warrants a keg on the lawn or fruity umbrella drinks, she has fun with what she serves.

She also knows that guests enjoy being offered the chance to try something new, so if it doesn't stretch the budget, she might add some alternatives to the usual bar staples (vodka, whiskey, gin, white wine, red wine, beer, and mixers). Tasty aperitifs (to serve before eating) include Campari, Lillet, or sherry. Digestifs, or after-meal drinks, always make for a nice cap on an evening. Some of our favorites: port, Amaro, and Sambuca. As for champagne, we don't think you need an "occasion" to pop a cork.

A lady makes an effort to learn the basics about wine. She knows spending

How a Great Hostess Does It

Katharine Graham, the legendary publisher of *The Washington Post,* was well known for her monthly dinner parties for up to fifty. Guests ran the gamut from heads of state to reporters, and there was never a dull moment when seated at one of her round tables. Graham's formula for success was delicious simplicity: homemade lasagna or grilled salmon was a usual main course. Her guests coveted her invitations and knew they would be well fed, both intellectually and gastronomically.

a lot of money isn't the only way to serve a good one, and that there are some wonderful, economical bottles to be had with a little research.

Lastly, a lady always has plenty of nonalcoholic drinks to offer guests—whether they are teetotalers, designated drivers, or just don't want to indulge. If her drink of the evening is something that can be served without alcohol, she serves it both ways. She never presses nondrinkers or asks why they're abstaining, and she offers plenty of other options so they don't feel like afterthoughts stuck sipping club soda.

There's always a chance that someone will shoot right by his or her alcohol limit without even braking. A lady keeps her eyes open and doesn't hesitate to intervene. She tactfully takes away the culprit's car keys and finds another solution to getting the guest home (or lets him or her sleep it off). A lady knows that any minor short-term inconvenience is eclipsed by the potential of letting someone drive drunk.

SETTING THE MOOD

Plates should be hot, hot, hot; glasses cold, cold, cold; and table decorations, low, low, low.

—ELSIE DE WOLFE

A lady knows it's not enough just to supply food, drinks, chairs, and people when she has a party. When she entertains, she thinks about the mood she wants to set for the event—everything from

Details, Details

In her role as U.S. ambassador to the United Nations, Madeleine Albright hosted countless meals and parties for diplomats from around the world. A stickler for details, she always checked each place card herself to make sure that her guests' names were spelled correctly. She would acknowledge the heritage of her guest of honor by trying to serve what might please him or her. If the Japanese ambassador was coming to breakfast, then the menu might include rice, fish, and raw eggs. Albright's technique often disarmed potential adversaries who, when they later found themselves across a negotiating table from her, wondered what had become of their gracious hostess.

the broad strokes to the little details. Nothing should feel contrived, but rather a natural part of the party's theme. The most important elements of setting the mood are music, lighting, decorative elements, and sometimes the food itself.

Some hints:

- Music should never be so loud as to hinder conversation, unless, of course, the occasion is a band performing or an evening of dancing. When music is merely a background for conversation, it's up to the hostess to select something that suits the crowd and the mood.

- Never underestimate the power of good lighting. At night, dimmer lighting is best; it creates intimacy and makes everyone look better. Dini: "A good friend of mine has a wonderful mood-setting device. No matter what the occasion, dinner for two, twelve, or fifty, she puts dozens of votive candles all over her house. There's something about the flickering light that puts guests at ease and sends a message to them to relax, that they're being taken care of."

- The littlest details often make the most impact. Flowers are a wonderful touch, be they simple daisies or exotic orchids. An artfully set table can also set the tone. For example: if, instead of cooking, a lady orders in Chinese food, she may set a table with chopsticks and red napkins, serve Chinese beer, and have her friends read the fortunes from their cookies aloud.

It's these small things that make her parties memorable and her guests delight in her thoughtfulness.

Big Night

Dini: "A friend of mine and her boyfriend decided to recreate the timbale scene from the movie *Big Night*. They spent two days making the incredible Italian meal and then invited all their friends over to help eat it. For them, two gourmands who love to eat and drink well, this was their way of sharing their passion with their closest friends. The mood all night was festive and exciting as we all anticipated, with great delight, each next course to come!"

TAKING IT ON THE ROAD

Of course, entertaining doesn't always mean a gala at the homestead, especially when you live in a studio apartment, have fussy roommates, or get anxious about cooking for more than yourself.

Survey Says

Some great mood-setting suggestions from the ladies we surveyed:

- "A relaxed atmosphere without a contrived topic is key."
- "Create good chemistry in a crowd. Read the mood and push it in the most appropriate direction, and initiate fun activities."
- "Create a calm, low-maintenance atmosphere where being with the guests and being a member of the party matters more than being the happy little frenetic hostess."
- "Placed enough food all over the house so everyone doesn't hover in one room."
- "Potluck! And paper plates! I can't handle all the prep and clean and have a good time, too!"

→

A lady can host a party just as smoothly somewhere else when the need arises, be it a banquet hall, a restaurant, or a favorite bar. The same rules apply, and it's still paramount that each guest feels her personal touch.

A few points to note:

For a smooth landing, a lady settles the bill before guests arrive to avoid confusion later on. Just as she'd refuse someone offering her a twenty as he left a party at her home, she's not tempted if people offer to chip in when the check comes. If she's organizing an event at which guests are expected to pay their own tabs, she makes it clear in advance so no one's caught unprepared.

A lady works closely with the location's staffers, letting them know the schedule, numbers of guests, and any special needs.

She arrives before her first guest to tip the maître d', hostess, coat checkers, or car parkers; charm the waiters (on whom she is depending to make the party go smoothly); set out place cards; decorate the table or check arrangements. After all, the party can't start without her!

WHEN GUESTS SPEND THE NIGHT

In keeping with her philosophy of entertaining, when a lady has houseguests, she will go that extra mile to make them feel at home. It doesn't matter if the "guest room" is really the living room with a couch sporting some sheets, or a luxury suite in its own wing. Making her guests feel comfortable and welcome is the goal. Some basics provided by any good hostess include: a clean room or sleeping area, an equally tidy bathroom, clean linens and towels, and a modicum of privacy. If a lady wants to go even further in her preparations, she can follow some of the suggestions our survey respondents provided:

- Leave a note in a picture frame by the bedside to let them know that nothing is off-limits—"get comfortable, open cabinets, put your feet up," etc.

- "Always go the extra mile! Otherwise, why bother?"

- "Champagne and interesting people are what I love. And good lighting!"

- "Candles, lots of finger foods, pillows to sit on the floor, fresh flowers, and fun people —that's all I need!"

- "Too much food, lots of different people, good music . . . and more food."

- "Enlisting people to help is always a good move. It gets everyone talking to each other, and inevitably we all end up laughing."

- Our respondents' most unusual entertaining tip? "Good friends, great music, good food, beach, full moon, drums, and a fire pit."

- Have lots of pillows and endless toiletries at their disposal, and try to create some privacy for them, even in a cramped space.
- Put soft, fragrant sheets on the bed and have a big country breakfast in the morning.
- Fill the medicine chest with supplies in case they forgot anything. Find out beforehand what they like for breakfast and anything they can't have, dietwise.
- Walk them around the kitchen and make sure they know they're welcome to anything there.
- A nightlight for the bathroom is key!
- Make or buy their favorite treat.

A Lady Is Also a Gracious Guest

When the tables turn, a lady is as good a guest as she is a hostess. She replies to invitations promptly and never asks who else is invited before doing so. She never accepts an invitation and then calls back to cancel because of a better offer or because she's changed her mind. (Illness or unforeseen obligations are the *only* acceptable excuses for canceling.) A lady never flakes out at the last minute!

A lady brings something for the host or hostess, be it wine, flowers, dessert, or even a book; what it is doesn't matter nearly as much as much as the gesture. Of course, if the occasion makes it inappropriate to bring a token of thanks, or it makes her hosts uncomfortable, a lady doesn't insist.

When she is a guest, a lady makes an effort to meet people she doesn't know, and she introduces guests she knows to one another. She behaves as she would want a guest of hers to behave: interested, polite, and engaging.

When appropriate, she will offer to assist the host, filling drink glasses, getting food out of the kitchen, or helping to clean up. If her host does not want her help, she does not press. It's not her party, after all.

Most important, a lady thanks the host for inviting her, whether with a call or a handwritten note, preferably the next day.

In an article she recently wrote for *Vanity Fair*, Brooke Astor, the famed philanthropist and writer and a true lady, aptly said:

> *When you are invited out to dinner, you are asked because your host or hostess likes you and thinks that you will add to the evening. You may be asked because you are an important person: a politician, a novelist, newly rich, a media tycoon, a beautiful woman, or a famous wit. But, whoever you are, there is still only one reason to be there: you are supposed to add to the evening. It is in the worst possible taste to be a sullen guest at a party even if you are seated between two bores, or between two people you have never been able to talk to. The host or hostess does not know your problems, nor were you intentionally put between two bores. Unless, possibly you did that to the hosts*

and they are taking their revenge. If this is the case, they won't get it if you appear to be having a good time. If your placement is bad unknowingly, then you are simply doing what is expected of you. My advice is, if you cannot add to the evening, you should stay at home and listen to the news . . . you can congratulate yourself that you are safely in bed.

SEVEN

romance: ladies in love, like . . . and lust

> *In olden days a glimpse of stocking*
> *Was looked on as something shocking—*
> *Now, heaven knows, anything goes.*
> —COLE PORTER

LET'S FACE it, times have changed. In today's world, anything goes between the sexes. Which is good. And bad. In the not-so-distant past, ladies were expected to be courted, wait for Mr. Right, and certainly not invite him in for a nightcap. Then came feminism and the sexual revolution, giving women more freedom to choose the whos, whens, hows, and whys of romance for themselves.

This empowerment has transformed romance into something less about bartering beauty and charm for financial security, and more about two people meeting each other's emotional (and/or physical) needs.

Fantastic, right? Well, sort of.

What we've been left with is a whole heap of confusion about how to interact with our "equals" without relinquishing those feminine qualities we may still like. Does the man always hold the door for a lady? Does a lady *ever* have sex on the first date? Is it appropriate to ask a man out? We could go on forever with the myriad of questions that have emerged in a time when *Sex and the City* and *Who Wants to Marry a Millionaire?* share the television airwaves with *7th Heaven* and *Touched by an Angel*.

Who wouldn't be confused?

Of course, what works for one person doesn't necessarily work for the next. But we assert that a lady conducts herself in love, like, and lust with a sensitivity and regard for others that seems woefully lacking in many in this era of—as the great Cole Porter portrayed it—anything goes. Rather than viewing romance and dating as some kind of planetary battle between Mars and Venus, our modern lady ventures forth into the dating game with an open mind, a considerate heart, and a desire to have a good time along the way.

RULES? WHAT RULES?

We were delighted to discover in our survey that 62 percent of our respondents had no rigid set of rules when it came to dating. Rather than treat all romantic prospects as if they were cut from the same cloth, the majority of our ladies recognized the uniqueness of individuals and situations. While 38 percent said they did subscribe to some rules of dating, we discovered upon examination that rather than abiding by rules like "Don't accept a date for Saturday evening after Wednesday," the essence of our ladies' codes had more to do with self-respect and consideration than keeping score and subtle manipulation.

For example:

- No games!
- No sex on the first date.
- Don't continue to go out with a man you don't like simply to have a date.
- Don't think you owe a man anything because he takes you out.
- Don't go out with married men.
- Never tolerate lies.
- Know when to back off.
- Always go out on at least two dates with someone; even if the first date was a bomb, give it a second chance because everyone can have an off night.
- Let a date know you had a good time.
- Don't forget your friends in the meantime.
- Have sex whenever you feel it's right.
- Don't "let" your date win—in a game, a sport, or an argument—just because it will make him/her feel good.

Rule One

If you're not being treated well, step back, run away, go! That would be the main rule in my dating book, and otherwise I think you have to enter into every situation with a fresh perspective. —SHOSHANNA LONSTEIN

A LADY KNOWS SHE'S A CATCH

As we've said before, a lady takes pride in the qualities she possesses—consideration for others, grace, dignity, generosity, and humor. No matter how you slice it, she's a catch. Sure, she may worry about never finding The One, but she doesn't sell herself short. And she certainly doesn't define herself by the romantic company she keeps. By being true to herself, she attracts the kinds of people she's interested in.

Survey Says . . .

96%: a lady may kiss on the first date

Only 6%: never make the first move

41%: have never asked a man out

46%: sex on the first date is okay for a lady

54%: a one-night stand is just fine for a lady

67%: kiss and tell their closest friends

91%: cheating is unacceptable

A lady approaches dating as the felicitous adventure it is, complete with its ups and downs, successes and failures, and pleasant surprises. That said, we all have days when insecurity rears its ugly head, so a lady knows never to embark on this adventure without a trusted group of guides—her friends—to make her laugh, remind her where her center is, and most importantly, that she is a catch.

She Knows How to Flirt

Whether a lady flirts like mad (with the UPS guy, her friends, people in line at the grocery store) or not at all, she understands that flirting is the mutually satisfying act of flattering banter, or as Brooke Astor put it, "sharing curiosity about one another."

Flirting is frivolous and fun. It makes you feel good. It makes your flirting partner feel good. But a lady is always careful of others' feelings. If her intentions are more lusty than friendly, she chooses her flirting partner carefully. She makes sure the person who has caught her eye is on the same page (i.e., interested and available), because it's her responsibility to gauge her company. Conversely, if the person she's flirting with shows an interest in taking the flirtation further than she'd like (say, a wedding chapel or the nearest hotel room) she changes her tone. A lady never leads someone on.

A lady is especially careful not to flirt in a way that might make her date or partner feel slighted or threatened. She never puts her own amusement above the feelings of others. (And do we really have to say that a lady never wields her charms on some unsuspecting target for the sole purpose of making her partner jealous?)

THE CHECK, PLEASE

When it comes to dealing with the check at the end of a date, a lady doesn't get flustered. She is not the sort to excuse herself to the ladies' room when she sees the waiter approaching (conveniently forcing her date to pay); nor does she cause a commotion by arm-wrestling for the check. A lady has her own guidelines regarding how to handle this situation—and they have as much to do with who she is as with her ability to pay. Here's a sampling of what our survey respondents had to say:

"Going dutch is a way to suggest you're open to covering your end, but if a date refuses, the polite thing to do is allow him or her to pay without a fuss." —Madeleine, Laguna Beach, CA

"I still believe a man should pay unless the woman asked the guy out. Then she should offer to pay or split the bill." —Dana, Brockton, MA

"If someone I don't know well asks me out, I tend to expect them to pick up the check. If it's a long-term relationship, then the desire to go out is mutual and I'll pay my own way." —Candice, Metairie, LA

"Whoever invites pays." —Beth, Brooklyn, NY, and Erica, Millbrook, NY

"I think that sharing the finances of a relationship helps to maintain balance in the relationship. I see absolutely no reason why a man should have to pay for more than the woman does." —Erin, Rosemont, PA

Our ladies recognize the need to clarify the nebulous, sometimes awkward, situations that can arise today when the check comes at the end of a date.

To be honest, women are in an enviable position. Traditionally, the man always picked up the tab (and many waiters still assume this when they bring the bill). It is rare that a woman will be taken to task for not paying her way. In knowing this, the power to change the dynamic belongs to us.

Here are a few guidelines for dealing with the tab:

- If asked on a first date, a lady need not feel obliged to pay her own way. It is fine for her to offer if she wants to.
- If she's invited on a date to a restaurant or a place that is very expensive (or beyond her means), she need not feel obliged to pay.
- A lady may offer to pay her share and even treat on occasion if a relationship develops. If nothing else, springing for drinks and movie tickets is a nice gesture.

- A lady always gauges her company. She never puts a date of modest means in the awkward position of having to stay home because she didn't consider their budget.
- When she does the inviting, she is prepared to pay the entire bill; she certainly pays for herself; and she accepts a date's offer to pay only if she wants to or it's appropriate (i.e., if her date makes a lot more money than she does, or if refusing might create a scene).
- When she's unsure who's picking up the tab, she doesn't order the most expensive item on the menu.

DOES A LADY MAKE THE FIRST MOVE?

In response to those who have declared it "against the rules" for a woman to ask a man out, we say: rubbish! It is no more inappropriate for a lady to ask someone out than it is for her to pick up the check once in a while. (Heck, some of the nicest guys might just be a bit intimidated by a woman as confident and together as our modern lady.) Rather than wait around for the cows to come home, some ladies choose to take the bull by the proverbial horns. The worst thing someone can say is "no thanks." (Heaven knows, for centuries men have faced that possibility.) Sometimes even when the answer is no, the outcome is a positive one.

Dini: "A few years ago I met a man, Jon, at a dinner party made up mainly of single people. He had barely made it because he had a terrible cold, but he was nice and smart and I enjoyed talking to him. Indeed, it was the first time in a long time that I had met someone I found so easy to talk to. During dinner it was clear that Jon was feeling horrible, so as soon as dessert ended, he excused himself and went home. A few days went by and I found myself thinking about him, so I called him and asked him out. He was very nice but declined, saying that he had a girlfriend. Naturally, I felt like a jerk for not checking with the friend who invited me first. As my stomach lurched and I raced to end the conversation, Jon said, 'We could have lunch instead.' Three years later, we're still friends."

LETTING 'EM DOWN EASY

We've all been there: the perfect sweetheart, but no chemistry . . . the charming, great conversationalist whose politics make you cringe . . . your best friend set you up, but you're not ready to get married after two dates! What's a lady to do?

When it comes to ending something, a lady is ultimately interested in sparing feelings. However, she is as honest, clear, and direct as possible so as not to dilute what she's saying with well-meaning compliments or regrets. As many of us know, mixed messages are often interpreted as hope.

No lady would put her own dread of confrontation ahead of clearing the air and preserving someone's dignity. This speaks particularly to those women who choose the cowardly and unkind "Don't answer the phone, don't call back" approach to ending courtships. As Amy in Connecticut wrote: "I handled it rather badly when I was younger. The old screening the calls, not calling back. I learned that it feels terrible when you're the one leaving messages and they don't call you back. Everyone deserves to hear the truth."

How might we put it? First, sound calm, poised, and nonjudgmental. Don't lay blame. Say something such as "I would rather we were just friends" or "This isn't working for me."

A lady is firm but never rude or cruel, no matter how annoying the rejected party might get. She might allow a certain amount of steam to be let off, but she will not tolerate rudeness, if for no other reason than she doesn't deserve it. If someone gets nasty or obsessive, she should feel perfectly comfortable walking away without any further apology and asking for no more contact.

WHEN A LADY IS SHOWN THE DOOR

Believe it or not, sometimes a lady is on the receiving end of a breakup. So, how does she handle it? With every bit of grace and dignity she can muster. She does not malign her ex to other people; she doesn't ask mutual friends to choose between them; and, most importantly, she does not beat herself up over a romance gone awry. (This is not to say some of us haven't hit the Ben & Jerry's or our favorite shoe store with a vengeance.) All kidding aside, just as we expect others to understand that "No thank you means no thank you," so should we. No calling and hanging up. No lingering at his favorite haunt. No dropping cookies off to remind him of what he's missing. (Ditto showing up in a trench coat wearing only lingerie underneath.) A lady knows the more quickly she moves on, the better. She looks for the positive, and if there's a lesson to be learned, she will make note of it and move on gracefully.

THE OUTER LIMITS: FRIENDS' EXES AND EXES' FRIENDS . . .

If a lady feels drawn to one of the aforementioned, she thinks long and hard before pursuing. Very long and hard. Is it worth it? Probably not, unless the person is the unanticipated love of her life. As a rule, a lady steers clear. Even if her friend says she won't mind her dating her ex, she may or may not mean it—even if she thinks she does. Plus, there's hardly an ex who wants to share a former flame with his or her friends.

Still, if a lady is sure she'd be passing up a possible soul mate, she behaves with discretion and respect, because there will be some trampled feelings. She and her new flame will think of ways to break the news that will soften the blow. They never flaunt their newfound happiness in front of the ex. While it's true that time heals all wounds, this is one wound that can make others feel *very* fragile. So a lady treads lightly.

. . . AND THE OTHERWISE COMMITTED

As our survey respondents asserted (and we concur), a lady steers clear of people who are married or in committed relationships. She never wants to be the person to destroy a relationship; nor does she want to be the accomplice or victim of a compulsive cheater.

However, some relationships just aren't meant to be, and it *is* possible that a lady's true soul mate may have taken a marital or cohabitative detour before their eyes ever met. If she believes it's true love, she will proceed with caution, discretion, and respect for the third party (spouse/partner) who, whether she knows it or not, is involved. A lady doesn't mind waiting however long it takes for her true love to be free. She knows it's better in the long run to start a relationship solidly and guilt-free, rather than building it on a foundation of deception.

Of course, a lady does not continue an illicit affair with a married or seriously involved person if she has no intention of taking it to the next level. She is evolved enough to know the difference between the carnal thrill of forbidden attraction and true love. If she wants a carnal thrill, she knows there are plenty of unattached people out there who would be happy to oblige. (If you're still not convinced, we recommend renting *Fatal Attraction.*)

LET'S TALK ABOUT SEX

Nookie, shagging, making love . . . whatever you call it, sometimes sex is the glue that keeps two people together. Sometimes it's the reason things don't work out. While some ladies wait to have sex until they're in a committed relationship, engaged, or married, others don't. Frankly, we believe sex is a private matter that belongs to the people having it. Provided a lady acts with respect for herself and others in romantic endeavors, she will never be in the wrong. Here are our three most basic tenets:

- A lady always has safe sex. These days, having sex is a serious, potentially life-threatening decision. If she can't talk about this with her partner, they have no business diving between the sheets.

- She makes decisions about intimacy with a clear head. She knows her limits when it comes to alcohol and spares herself and others the embarrassment and awkwardness that often follows an encounter fueled by too many cocktails.

- When a partner suggests something she's not ready for or "into," she is confident enough to decline politely and firmly. As long as she's treated with respect, she does everything she can to avoid making the other person feel bad for asking.

COMMUNICATION, COMMUNICATION, AND OH YES, COMMUNICATION

The key to any good relationship, on-screen or off, is communication, respect, and I guess you have to like how the other person smells . . ."

—*SANDRA BULLOCK*

A lady knows the value of communication in her romantic relationships, as in most other things. She does not rely on someone else's mind-reading abilities to get her through. That is to say, if all she wants is a fling, then she says so—respectfully and sensitively. If she's looking for a relationship to blossom into something long-term, she needs to behave in a way that cannot be misinterpreted. For example, a lady thinks twice about what she's getting into before hopping into the sack with her best buddy—which could be a suddenly awkward friendship, or a love she didn't have in mind.

After that, all a lady can hope for is the same kind of respect and honesty from her partner.

DISCRETION

I think discretion—a sense of privacy—is really important. I am taken aback when people discuss things of an intimate nature in the kind of detail I don't think should leave a gynecologist's office . . . Please, I don't want to know!

—*CANDICE BERGEN*

Just as she eschews gossiping about others, a lady exercises polite discretion in affairs of an intimate nature. Whether she's casually dating, in a serious relationship, or in the wake of a one-night stand, she knows implicitly that what goes on between two people belongs to them first and foremost.

For celebrities who are hounded by press and paparazzi looking for juicy peeks into their personal lives, the protection of privacy has proven quite difficult. But many ladies, including Julia Roberts, Jennifer Aniston, Brooke Shields, Sandra Bullock, Reese Witherspoon, and Sarah Jessica Parker, have managed to create a protective boundary around their private lives, often offering only the minimal confirmation of a relationship followed by a polite and firm "I don't like to talk about my personal life." Julia Roberts has been known to reply to inquiring interviewers that if she starts talking about her beau's wonderfulness, she could talk for a week; hence, it's better that she says nothing at all. It's those ladies in the public eye who resist the temptation to exploit their private lives for the sake of getting ink that we spotlight as inspiration.

If she *must* share: when it comes to choosing her audience, a lady remembers that some people are more modest than others. And she knows when too much information is just that. While it's fun to trade girl-talk with friends, a lady reserves the most intimate details for people she trusts will not view her disclosure as vulgar, crude, or inappropriate.

WHEN A LADY GOES "STEADY"

Sometimes we meet a special someone who compels us to take ourselves out of the dating game. When a lady enters into a committed relationship, she approaches it with the same kind of regard she does her friendships ... and then some. A lady recognizes that relationships need nurturing and occasional sacrifices, and she is not one to take her partner for granted. She knows that every relationship requires honesty, respect, compromise, appreciation, patience, and a whole bunch of hard work. Beyond that, we believe every partnership has its own unique recipe for success, and we are happy to leave the finer points of a lady's committed relationship, with all its infinite variables, to her and her partner to sort out.

EIGHT

social responsibility: a lady

pays attention

*Realize that life is glorious and you have no business
taking it for granted. Care so deeply about its goodness
that you want to spread it around. Take the money you
would have spent on beers in a bar and give it to charity.
Work in a soup kitchen. Tutor a seventh grader.*
—ANNA QUINDLEN, *A Short Guide to a Happy Life*

WE HEAR all the time that the world is getting smaller. We are
better informed and more in touch than we have been at any time
in human history. Being bombarded with indiscriminate barrages
of information seems only to make us more detached. Culturally,
we are overfocused on fame, fortune, and conspicuous consumption, and increasingly cynical about our own capacity to make a
difference. In spite of this, a lady remains socially aware and
active—she knows that to do less is a self-fulfilling prophecy,
that apathy toward her community invites its apathy toward her.

We have said many times that a lady pays attention to the world around her, in consideration for others and how her actions affect them. This applies in a broader sense; just as she feels responsibility to the people in her immediate orbit and community, a lady keeps her eyes and heart open to the larger world out there.

This manifests itself in both large and small ways. Whether taking the time to help a woman get her stroller up a flight of stairs; making sure to recycle; donating money or time to a cause she believes in; or raising her children to be the kind of people who will make the world a better place, a lady gives back. As Billie Jean King once said, "The most important words that have helped me in life—when things have gone right, or when things have gone wrong—are 'accept responsibility.' It's everyone's responsibility to lead, to honor and to fight for everyone's basic rights, for equality." Of the two hundred ladies we surveyed, 91 percent of them were actively involved in social causes through volunteering. And a full 100 percent of our respondents who had volunteered said that they got great personal rewards from doing so.

WHY SHE DOES IT

We've learned from firsthand experience that giving back is its own reward. The power of doing good is the positive effect it has not just on others but on ourselves. Noelle is an adult literacy tutor, teaching two men from Guatemala how to read so they can get better jobs. Dini is the cofounder and president of Love Heals, the Alison Gertz Foundation for AIDS Education, which provides HIV/AIDS education for young people.

As actress Julianna Margulies told us, when Sojourn—a shelter in Los Angeles for women and children—asked her for a donation, she decided to see it with her own eyes: "I went there and met them and was blown away by the people who run these shelters. So I just started getting involved, bringing the kids crayons and paper and paints and arts-and-crafts stuff. I realized how such a small gesture can go such a long way."

SOCIAL RESPONSIBILITY BEGINS AT HOME

Being socially responsible is not always the grand gesture—it can sometimes be as simple as separating the plastic from the metal recyclables. Some basics:

- Recycling and reusing (96 percent of our survey respondents do, whether legally required or not)
- Carpooling or using mass transit when possible
- Choosing products with minimal packaging or made from degradable or recycled materials
- Giving unneeded items such as clothes and home furnishings to charitable organizations rather than throwing them away
- Being a conscientious consumer (i.e., supporting businesses that do good works and/or boycotting manufactur-

ers who pollute, exploit, or advertise on programs that you think are socially irresponsible)

- Voting in local, state, and national elections for people who stand for what you believe in (of our survey respondents, 93 percent said they vote, which isn't remarkable until you remember the national average is below 50 percent)

FIGHTING THE GOOD FIGHT

To many women, and I am one of them, it is extraordinarily difficult to care about anything enough to cause disagreement or unpleasant feelings, but I have come to the conclusion that this must be done for a time until we can prove our strength and demand respect for our wishes.

—*ELEANOR ROOSEVELT, ON SUFFRAGE*

It isn't always easy to do the right thing. In fighting for what we believe in, we may find ourselves losing the popularity contest, or under the glare of klieg lights. But even if it requires behaving more as a fighter than as peacekeeper, our beliefs are too important not to stand up for.

As Eleanor Roosevelt said, causing disagreement may not be pleasant, but it's often necessary. In 1939, when black opera singer Marian Anderson was barred from performing at Washington, D.C.'s Constitution Hall because of her race, Roosevelt resigned from the Daughters of the American Revolution, the group that owned the hall. The first lady then went a step further and arranged for Anderson to sing instead at the Lincoln Memorial. Roosevelt was validated when a crowd of seventy-five thousand turned out to hear the legendary Anderson perform that Easter Sunday.

In 1973 the twenty-nine-year-old Billie Jean King courageously stepped forward on behalf of another then-disenfranchised group, female athletes, and accepted a challenge to play three sets of tennis against Bobby Riggs. Riggs had stated on record that no female, no matter how good, could beat a man, and had been baiting King to play him for months. She'd always politely declined, but after Riggs beat Margaret Court, who was ranked first in the world, King decided she had to accept the challenge. "I had no choice," she said. "I didn't feel women were accepted as athletes yet. Title IX [the federal ban on gender discrimination in education programs, including sports] had just passed, and I could see people [looking] for an excuse to backtrack. I wanted to change the hearts and minds of people to match the legislation we had just gotten in place."

King not only cleaned the court with Riggs, she went on to cofound the Women's Sports Foundation, which funneled money into programs promoting gender equity in sports; created *Women's Sports* magazine; and started the Billie Jean King Foundation to promote equal opportunity outside of sports. As she explained it, "Everything I do is about equal opportunity. Race, gender, sexual orientation. Let's get over it. Let's celebrate our differences."

Time vs. Money

The great thing about giving back is that everyone has something to offer, be it money or time or even knowledge. Of course, no one is expected to give what she cannot spare. If her time is too precious to volunteer, a lady may make charitable donations. If money is tight and she can't give any away, then she might contribute a couple of hours a week or month to helping someone or an organization she cares about.

Money Well Spent

Ladies, if they're [financially] lucky enough to be charitable are charitable, and they are evolved and involved. —Paula Zahn

Financial guru and best-selling author Suze Orman is a proponent of donating money to charitable causes, no matter how little the amount—and 69 percent of our survey respondents agreed.

146

In her book *The 9 Steps to Financial Freedom*, Orman expressed this sentiment:

> *Beyond a shadow of a doubt, I now know the following principle is true: We experience prosperity, true financial freedom, when our actions with respect to money are karmic, or righteous, actions—that is, actions of generosity, actions of offering.*
>
> *Money flows through our lives just like water—at times plentiful, at times a trickle. I believe that each one of us is, in effect, a glass, in that we can only hold so much; after that, the water—or the money—just goes down the drain. Some of us are larger glasses, some of us are smaller, but we all have the capacity to receive plenty more than we need if we allow it. When you make an offering, the glass will be filled again and again and again.*

A lady knows that, besides giving money, she can also put the money she

Christiane Amanpour Throws Down the Gauntlet

At a journalism awards banquet recently, CNN foreign correspondent Christiane Amanpour made news herself. Lamenting the shrinking news budgets at network operations—which have made news shows dependent on ratings over content and have especially curtailed the amount of international coverage shown in the U.S.—Amanpour said:

> *If we have no respect for our viewers, then how can we have any respect for ourselves and what we do? . . . The bottom line is that there are a lot of dedicated and great journalists who work either in the U.S. or abroad, who, like me, are extremely, extremely worried—and that's an understatement—about the direction of our business.*

→

It's now or never for our profession. We've got to get a grip. We've got to start being journalists again, instead of catering or pandering to what we think the viewers want.

We applaud the courage it took for Amanpour to challenge the status quo, and so did her peers, who gave her a standing ovation. Let's see what happens.

already spends to good use. There are many different ways to give money to organizations, as some of our survey respondents pointed out: Working Assets, a long-distance carrier, gives a portion of all its profits to social causes; companies such as American Express, Body Shop, Avon, Tom's of Maine, Ben & Jerry's, Newman's Own, and many, many others give a percentage of dollars spent to charity. You can even spend a few extra cents on breast cancer–awareness postage stamps that go toward research for the cure. We believe that researching socially responsible companies is time well spent.

GIVING TIME

Giving one's time is just as personally gratifying as giving money, if not more. In many cases, a lady's time, service, or expertise can be more valuable than a monetary contribution. For example, if she's an attorney, she can offer her services pro bono—most nonprofits can't afford top-rate lawyers, but what could be more needed than their services? Likewise, a graphic artist can donate her time to design newsletters and flyers for a local convalescent home or political group; a college student can give a week of her summer break to build houses with an organization such as Habitat for Humanity; or a health-care professional can give a few hours a month to a local free clinic.

Public Figures Do Good

You must be the change you wish to see in the world. —*Mohandas Gandhi*

If she is in a po\sition to influence people, a lady does so on behalf of causes she supports. Celebrities have unique power, particularly in our current culture of fame and fortune. The media obsesses over stars' wardrobes, romances, breakups, diets, and almost any other aspects of their lifestyles, dissecting every word they say. When celebrities recognize their power and use their influence for the betterment of others, they are exercising social responsibility of the highest order.

We're not talking about people who merely safety-pin a red or pink ribbon to their evening clothes at a Hollywood awards ceremony, but about those who

A Mississippi Laundress Gives It All Back

To us, no one better exemplifies social consciousness and generosity than the late Oseola McCarty. A Hattiesburg, Mississippi, laundress, McCarty donated $150,000—nearly her entire life savings—to the University of Southern Mississippi in 1995 to give young women the opportunity for education and advancement that she didn't have as a black woman in the 1920s South. While she had always yearned for an education, McCarty was forced to drop out of school in the sixth grade to help support her family. For seventy-five years, she washed and ironed the clothes of some of Hattiesburg's most prominent citizens, always depositing—but never withdrawing—whatever was left over into the bank after she paid her bills.

The gift was the largest ever made to the university by an African American, and as far as the eighty-seven-year-old was concerned, she wished it could have been more.

"I just want the scholarship to go to some child who needs it, to whoever is not able to help their children," McCarty said. "I'm too old to get an education, but they can.

"I can't do everything," she continued, "but I can do something to help somebody. And what I can do, I will do. I wish I could do more."

truly give of their time, money, and heart in a way that makes people pay attention.

Susan Sarandon routinely draws attention to causes that are important to her. She marches for stricter gun-control laws, reproductive rights, and AIDS, and acts as special representative for UNICEF. Nor is she afraid of potential repercussions when she stands up for her beliefs. As she put it, "I can't imagine not being active. When people ask me if I'm worried about my career being affected, I always say that it's like worrying if your slip is showing when you're fleeing a burning building."

We could devote an entire book to lauding public figures who use their influence and stature to make a difference. Here are a handful of ladies we love and the good work they do:

- Country singer Faith Hill established the Faith Hill Family Literacy Project in honor of her father who, as one of thirteen children, had to go to work before he could learn to read. As she explained it: "Money is a wonderful thing and can bring awareness or, in the case of medical research, bring you closer to finding a cure. But writing a check can be so easy. This feels like the right thing for me to do. I didn't just want to write a check and say 'see ya.'"

- World Championship and Olympic gold medalist soccer star Mia Hamm takes being a role model seriously. The Mia Hamm Foundation has two missions: to promote girls' participation in sports and to increase awareness about bone marrow disease and raise money for research, in memory of her brother Garrett who died from the illness.

- NBC *Today* show cohost Katie Couric used her show to bring attention to colorectal cancer, the disease that took the life of her husband, Jay Monahan. A month after his death, Couric broadcast her own colonoscopy to underscore the importance of early detection.

- Singer and hip-hop artist Lauryn Hill founded the Refugee Project, a foundation whose programs target at-risk, inner-city youths aged ten to fourteen. For two weeks each summer, a hundred youths go to Camp Hill, then take part in a mentoring program once a month for the rest of the year. Hill also has held concerts to benefit Haitian refugees, as well as participating in relief projects in Africa. She explains her commitment to helping others: "God gave me a certain amount of influence for a reason. I wanted to know that what I was doing was really touching people's lives. If not me, who else?"

- Biologist Dr. Mathilde Krim was a cancer research scientist at the beginning of the HIV/AIDS epidemic. Seeing the need to both study the virus and speak out against the hysteria and misinformation about the disease, in 1983 she cofounded the national organization AmFAR (American Foundation for AIDS Research), of which she remains chairwoman. Since its inception, AmFAR has raised over $100 million for experimental AIDS research projects, many of which have become the treatments that are now standard.

- Gossip columnist Liz Smith is a longtime champion of the Literacy Volunteers of America, for which she has raised $20 million to teach illiterate adults how to read. In her national column, she tirelessly promotes causes she deems worthy, using her power and breadth of influence to open people's minds.

- Supermodel Christy Turlington is the chairwoman of the International Committee for Intercambios Culturales of El Salvador, helping post–civil war El Salvador catch up with the technology and education standards of other countries. She is also an antismoking activist and the poster girl for *STOP!*, a new magazine dedicated to quitting smoking, as well as one of the faces of Fashion Targets Breast Cancer.

- Former first lady Rosalynn Carter has long fought hard for public recognition of mental illness and the unfair stigmatization of the mentally ill. She also works with the

Carter Center, which seeks to prevent and resolve conflicts and enhance freedom for democracy. She regularly gives her time to Habitat for Humanity, a nonprofit organization that has built over a hundred thousand houses for the underprivileged worldwide. She and her husband, former president Jimmy Carter, were both awarded the Presidential Medal of Freedom in 1999 because they have, said President Bill Clinton, "done more good things for more people in more places than any other couple on the face of the earth."

Then there's a lady who's in a class by herself: Oprah Winfrey. In the last ten years she has not only used her power, wealth, and influence to fund literacy programs, promote positive body image, enlighten Americans about important social issues like teen drug abuse, racism, sexism, deadbeat dads, single motherhood, and more, she has also turned her television show and magazine, *O*, into platforms to spotlight the great works of others all over the country—people who ordinarily don't get the recognition they deserve. Among her other acts of social responsibility, Oprah has also started the world's largest piggy bank, matching donations sent in by viewers to send disadvantaged kids to college. So far, the fund has raised over $1 million. She also took a brave stand against the tobacco and diet industries by not accepting cigarette or diet-program ads in her magazine. On a daily basis, Oprah

Two Champions of Giving Back: Brooke Astor and Irene Diamond

No ladies of wealth and social status have better used their positions to do good than Brooke Astor and Irene Diamond. And they've both done so with immeasurable grace and style.

Placed at the helm of the Vincent Astor Foundation by her late husband in 1961, Brooke Astor had instructions to spend all of its nearly $200 million endowment and to have fun doing it. She set three principles: focus on New York, initiate "people-based projects," and give money to projects that she could see herself. As a result, New York City's financially strapped public

→

encourages all of us to be better human beings.

Celebrities are not the only ladies of influence who deserve citation. In business, there are many who have not let the bottom line dictate everything. These ladies recognize that giving back is good business. Cosmetics queen Estée Lauder was among the earliest businesswomen to put her company's name—and a percentage of its profits—behind breast cancer research. Andrea Jung, CEO of Avon, has followed suit. The innovative ladies of the TV channel and website Oxygen, a media conglomerate whose partners include Oprah Winfrey, Marcy Carsey, and CEO Geraldine Laybourne, launched a micro-loan program to help women start up their own businesses.

IT'S NEVER TOO LATE

Some people don't get involved in giving back until they have reached a stage in their life when they feel they can afford either the time or the money. Others give back in whatever way they can when they can, albeit sometimes sporadically. For yet others, social responsibility comes as a result of experiencing a life change—anything from the loss of a friend or family member to illness to the birth of a child or even a chance encounter that raises awareness. This call to take action can come in any form, but most important is that it comes at all.

For actress Meryl Streep, the birth of her first child gave her a new consciousness of the world and a renewed sense of responsibility. "This child will have to get us into the next century," she said. "His generation will have to deal with problems of survival that our generation never even thought of: pollution, depletion of natural resources, population control." Streep became an outspoken opponent of nuclear arms and the use of dangerous pesticides, and an advocate for causes including women's reproductive rights and pediatric AIDS research.

library system was given new life; the Metropolitan Museum of Art built a Ming Dynasty courtyard; the interior of Harlem's Apollo Theater was restored, and much more. Astor has been much more than a check writer, often going to visit the beneficiaries of her generosity. Her proudest achievement came after she visited the bare apartments of two Queens families who had successfully moved from homelessness to private housing but couldn't afford furniture. The result: the Furnish a Future program, which since 1990 has helped almost twelve thousand poor families furnish new quarters.

Irene Diamond was always an iconoclast, and the recipients of her largesse know this better than anyone. A story edi-

→

155

tor in the 1930s, Diamond was responsible for discovering and cultivating such hit films as *Casablanca, Dark Victory,* and *The Maltese Falcon.* She later moved to New York and married a young businessman, Aaron Diamond, whose real estate business brought them great wealth. In 1984 Aaron and Irene were walking on the beach, and he told her what he wanted her do with their fortune after his death: give 40 percent to medical research, 40 percent to minority education, and 20 percent to the arts.

Upon his passing, Irene began not just to donate the money but also to initiate programs where none existed previously. These included cocreating the Funders' Collaborative for Gun Violence Prevention (which

→

THE ULTIMATE SOCIAL RESPONSIBILITY: MOTHERHOOD

The most important contribution any lady can make to society is to love and care and nurture her own children to become the best humans they can be.

—LINDA STASI, COLUMNIST, NEW YORK POST

A lady puts her children first, no matter whether she's a homemaker or a CEO. The *hows* of raising of children are as individual as how you take your coffee, and we are the last people to tell anyone how to do it. But when a lady makes the commitment to being a parent, she enters into a lifelong relationship that she puts ahead of all others and makes her utmost responsibility. As Jacqueline Kennedy Onassis once said, "If you bungle raising your children, I don't think whatever else you do well matters very much."

A lady knows that children learn by example. And the lessons a lady imparts to her children are as much unspoken as they are articulated: do as I say *and* as I do.

Of course, being a mother is not easy—especially if a woman works, as more of us do than not. Women are taken to task for their choices, whether they are stay-at-home moms or try to balance a career and motherhood. How does a lady handle it all? With as much grace as possible and often a lot of guilt and too little sleep. As Madeleine Albright said, "I think guilt is kind of a middle name for women who have a career and children and a husband."

When push comes to shove, a lady is there for her children, even if it means she makes up for it later at work. She somehow finds time for both parent-teacher conferences and sales meetings; she puts soccer games and school plays before work parties, knowing that being a good parent is a one-shot deal and she won't get those years back. (There will always be another work meeting!) Let's face it, no gold watch or plaque is ever given with as much love and pride as a child's strung-pasta necklace or finger-painted picture.

helped fund the Million Mom March) and fighting AIDS. In 1988, after seeing how slowly AIDS research and prevention efforts were progressing, she made them her priority, donating $51 million to efforts against it. She established the Aaron Diamond AIDS Research Center, headed by Dr. David Ho, the preeminent doctor in the field and *Time* magazine's 1996 Man of the Year, who created the current standard AIDS treatments and is currently working on a vaccine. Far from being uninvolved, Irene is known for dropping in on recipients of her generosity, as she did one day on a dance program in a homeless shelter, "to see where my money is going."

Mothers First, Actresses Second

When my agent calls me with a job offer, the first question I ask is, "Where is it filming?" If it's other than in L.A., most of the time I say I can't do it, because it will upset my family schedule.

—JAMIE LEE CURTIS

I try to balance the intense drive to grow creatively and the incredible resentment of anything that interferes with my child's care. Guilt is an inherent part of being a working mother.

—UMA THURMAN

A lady also does more than show up: she is deeply involved in her children's lives, from what they watch, read, and listen to, to whom they spend time with, to being there to answer the questions that only a parent can.

A lady knows that in no other job are the challenges as big but the rewards greater: the love, respect, and friendship of her children and seeing them turn out well.

In her book *Ten Things I Wish I'd Known Before I Went Out into the Real World*, Maria Shriver writes about being in Cuba to interview Fidel Castro for a television special the week before her eldest daughter's first day of nursery school. After postponing the interview several times, Castro met with the NBC team to announce another delay. Almost without thinking, Shriver blurted out that she had to be home to take her daughter to school. Her producer was horrified, but without skipping a beat, Castro said, "Take your daughter to school. I'll be ready next Saturday morning." When Shriver returned to Cuba to shoot "one

of the most fascinating interviews of my career," the first thing
Castro said to her was "How was the first day of school?"

Social responsibility comes in many forms. A lady's consciousness of her world is what leads her to action—whatever shape
that action takes. "All of us want to do well," Anna Quindlen has
written. "But if we do not do good, too, then doing well will never
be enough."

A lady knows doing well is never as meaningful when she is
not also doing good.

in closing: the power of a lady

BEING A lady is an "art" and not a birthright. It's something that has to be earned. It's about paying attention and aspiring to do the right thing—even when others don't. That's what sets a lady apart from the crowd. It's what garners her respect and admiration and inspires all of us to keep trying. That is the *power* of being a lady.

Any woman can be a lady—and, we believe, everyone should want to be one.

The challenges and pressures of life in the modern world are very real. To rise above the fray and do what's right takes great strength, confidence, and most of all, the ability to see beyond yourself—especially in a world that consistently rewards self-advancement at nearly any cost. That's why we believe any woman who achieves that special balance deserves to be recognized: as a lady.

This book is certainly not the last word on being a lady. Rather, it is the first

We're eager to hear from you. If you have questions, arguments, opinions, or stories that you'd like to share, please go to www. theladybook.com.

word. We hope that it begins a dialogue—with your friends, your family, and your community; even within yourself. Take the advice of the ladies who spoke to you here—and remember the power lies in you. The next time you want to pay a woman a compliment, try calling her a lady. We guarantee you'll put a smile on her face.

a lady is . . .

". . . someone who shows grace under pressure, can assert herself without being perceived as harsh, who gets the job done without sacrificing femininity."

–Paula Zahn, Anchor, FoxTV News

". . . [a woman] who lives an honorable life, [and] has a sense of priorities, of social responsibility . . . I think paying attention is really critical . . . I think someone who behaves elegantly is someone who pays great attention.   –Candice Bergen

". . . a woman with grace, dignity, style, intelligence, finesse and integrity. I love the term lady and I always refer to my women creative people as 'ladies."

–Nina DiSesa, CEO, McCann-Erickson NY

". . . a woman who possesses: poise (meaning: ability to think on one's feet, keep it together under pressure or stress, wear a poker face when necessary—especially in business); the ability to find a win-win solution or scenario (aikido principle, I think, about both winning and not winning at someone else's expense); the wherewithall not to fall into the bitterness trap—especially making men the enemy or placing all the blame on men; compassion; generosity (being a mentor after one's accomplished at least some of her goals and doing some good for someone after someone else did right by her); and, finally, one I struggle with a lot: the capacity to know when saying nothing is better (e.g., when a smart-alecky quip will detract from your strength for the price of a cheap laugh").

–Sherri Rifkin, Director,
Consumer Marketing Online, Oxygen Media

". . . . is the woman who pauses and reflects. Haste does not make a lady. Low blood pressure makes a lady. A woman who sees the yellow light, then runs across Park Avenue to make it is not, to me, a lady. What is she scampering after?"

–Alex Kuczynski, media reporter, *New York Times*

". . . [someone who] rises above some disagreeable circumstance—as in, she doesn't let a colleague's back-stabbing get to her; she elegantly rises above the fray, refrains from office gossip, and floats in the above-it-all clouds with an enigmatic smile on her face and the feel of a buffer zone around her that will protect her from those who would cause her harm or discomfort."

–Betty Rothbart, author, *Multiple Blessings*

". . . secure in herself and whose positive outlook is infectious to all those around her."   —Alanna, Los Angeles, CA

". . . confident, well-mannered, articulate, and considerate."
                    —Madeleine, Hollywood, CA

". . . maintains the old-fashioned sense of class and graciousness with a modern sense of independence and intelligence."
                    —Ellen, Sherman Oaks, CA

". . . a person who speaks her mind but doesn't feel the need to flaunt or overexert herself to get her point across. She is confident about her manners, has a sense of style and poise but she is not a slave to others' opinions of her. She is kind, quick-witted, bright, compassionate, hard-working, savvy."
                    —Kearney, New York City

". . . a person who is not embarrassed to be a strong woman with strong opinions . . . someone who is comfortable in her own skin and likes herself . . . someone that isn't defined by her man or mate . . . someone that is caring, thoughtful and generous of herself . . . someone who never forgets who she is, where she came from, and who her true friends are."   —Heidi, Somerville, MA

". . . a woman with an air of confidence, an ability to maintain dignity under all circumstances and the intelligence to decipher appropriate behavior and attitude for various situations."

—Arianna, West Palm Beach, FL

". . . someone with dignity, who is gracious, mannerly, composed, and self-possessed—those are the external traits, the ones we observe most easily. But a true lady is also honorable, courteous, and kind."   —Candice, Metairie, LA

". . . quite different from my definition of a woman. A lady is an individual who seems to have this innate presence that any person in her company immediately recognizes as something special. Something that is classy, graceful, and understated, but so present in the individual that one has to acknowledge this "thing" that she has."   —Monica, Arlington, MA

". . . always appropriate and kind, without ever being stuffy."

—Samantha, Hollywood, CA

". . . filled with confidence, so much so that she has no need for ostentation, grandstanding, one-upmanship, or self-promotion. A lady is at peace with herself, so everything she does springs from the purest of intentions. Even a woman with no style can be a lady, for a true lady makes her own unique style. A woman in rags with a fourth-grade education can be a lady. I've seen homeless women who have more inner resolve and dignity than some of the wealthiest, well-kept and well-educated women."

—Jada, Concord, NH

". . . someone who knows and likes herself so well that she carries herself with dignity and grace at all times; a woman who can say so much with just a few words, or even no words at all; a woman who is never loud or obvious." —Anonymous

". . . a person who speaks her mind while respecting what's on others' minds; someone who makes you feel at ease in her presence; someone who makes you feel welcome in her home."

—Nicole, Cambridge, MA

". . . a confident, self-aware, poised woman with class, manners, self-respect, and the presence and strength to stand up for herself and her beliefs." —Erica, Millbrook, NY

". . . a person who has manners and common sense, and treats all people with respect." —Clare, San Diego, CA

". . . assertive, self-assured, confident and yet still allows a man to be a gentleman." —Anonymous

". . . someone who treats others as she would like to be treated—always. A woman who commands respect because she is always willing to pay it to others."   —Erin, Rosemont, PA

". . . kind, considerate, and thoughtful . . . but not selfless to a fault. A lady knows the meaning of the word balance. She can help other people feel special while keeping her own needs a priority. She is intelligent and knows it, but can still laugh at herself and find joy in the world around her."   —Donna, Columbia, CT

". . . a female who possesses a strong sense of control—control over her own emotions, the decisions she makes, and her effect on others."   —Amy, Brooklyn, NY

". . . someone who can enter any situation and participate in a way that leaves everyone else feeling as if their life has just been touched by someone special."   —Paige, Sagaponack, NY

". . . a woman who has mastered the balance of power and grace."
                    —Tamara, Brooklyn, NY

". . . gracious, able to make all those around her feel comfortable at all time, someone who others aspire to become, someone who makes those around her feel special."—Celina, Boston, MA

". . . comfortable and secure in most situations . . . who isn't nervous, loud, rude, or self-centered in social situations . . . an accomplished yet humble person." —Adriana, New York City

". . . aware of her surroundings and considerate of the comfort level of those around her, at the same time being confident and at ease with who she is."   —Jean, West Hollywood, CA

". . . a cool chick, who has class, but who can play with the boys, and who can slip out of her dress and get into some old jeans and play pool."   —Mary, San Diego, CA

". . . happy and confident in who she is and is eager to share the world with others. She is considerate and kind and has the ability to make others feel great about themselves."

          —Sarah, Los Angeles, CA

bibliography

Books

Anderson, Sherry Ruth, and Patricia Hopkins. *The Feminine Face of God: The Unfolding of the Sacred in Women.* New York: Bantam, 1992.

Bartlett, John, ed. *Bartlett's Familiar Quotations,* Sixteenth Edition. New York: Little, Brown, 1992.

Bergen, Candice. *Knock Wood.* New York: Ballantine, 1990.

Berry, Carmen Renee, and Tamara Traeder. *Girlfriends: Invisible Bonds, Enduring Ties.* Wildcat Canyon Press, 1995.

Blackman, Ann. *Seasons of Her Life: A Biography of Madeleine Korbel Albright.* New York: Scribner, 1998.

Brinkley, Douglas. *Rosa Parks.* New York: Viking, 2000.

Goodman, Ellen, and Patricia O'Brien. *I Know Just What You Mean.* New York: Simon & Schuster, 2000.

Harris, Lynn. *Breakup Girl to the Rescue!: A Superhero's Guide to Love, and Lack Thereof.* Boston: Back Bay, 2000.

Keough, Pamela Clark. *Audrey Style.* New York: HarperCollins, 1999.

Klein, Edward. *Just Jackie: Her Private Years.* New York: Ballantine, 1998.

Leach, Maria, ed. *The Importance of Being a Wit: The Insults of Oscar Wilde.* London: Michael O'Mara, 1997.

Maychick, Diana. *Meryl Streep: The Reluctant Superstar.* New York: St. Martin's, 1984.

Maychick, Diana. *Audrey Hepburn: An Intimate Portrait.* New York: Citadel, 1996.

Moats, Alice-Leone. *No Nice Girl Swears.* Oxford, England: Past Times, 1997 (Reprint/Revise), originally published in 1933 by Cassell & Co.

Morton, Andrew. *Diana: Her True Story.* New York: Simon & Schuster, 1997.

Orman, Suze. *The 9 Steps to Financial Freedom.* New York: Crown, 1997.

Post, Peggy, ed. *Emily Post's Etiquette.* New York: HarperCollins, 1997.

Quindlen, Anna. *A Short Guide to a Happy Life.* New York: Random House, 2000.

Rossellini, Isabella. *Some of Me.* New York: Random House, 1997.

Shriver, Maria. *Ten Things I Wish I'd Known Before I Went Out into the Real World.* New York: Warner, 2000.

Smith, Liz. *Natural Blonde.* New York: Hyperion, 2000.

Tapert, Annette, and Diana Edkins. *The Power of Style.* New York: Crown, 1994.

Tapert, Annette, and Ellen Horan. *The Power of Glamour.* New York: Crown, 1998.

Washington, George. *Rules of Civility: The 110 Precepts That Guided Our First President in War and Peace,* ed. Richard Brookhiser. New York: Free Press, 1997.

Wiesen Cook, Blanche. *Eleanor Roosevelt: 1884–1933.* New York: Penguin, 1993.

Young Stewart, Marjabelle. *The New Etiquette: Real Manners for Real People in Real Situations—An A to Z Guide.* New York: St. Martin's, 1997.

Magazines

Astor, Brooke. "The Lost Art of Flirting." *Vanity Fair.* February 2000.

Astor, Brooke. "Please, Call Me Mrs. Astor." *Vanity Fair.* June 1999.

Biography. "Top 10 Beauties of the Decade." November 1999.

Bosworth, Patricia. "Rebel with a Purse." *Vanity Fair.* December 2000.

Bush, Vanessa. "On the Beach with Jamie Lee Curtis." *Life.* March 2000.

Cheever, Susan. "Architectural Digest Visits Candice Bergen." *Architectural Digest.* October 1999.

Coyne, Kate. "Real Beauty 2000." *Good Housekeeping.* January 2000.

Gandee, Charles. "The Look of the Century. What We Wore Now. Highlights of the High Life. 1990s." *Vogue.* November 1999.

Glenn-Dowling, Claudia. "Heroes of the Year." *Life.* January 1999.

Griffiths, John. "Sheer Sandra." *InStyle.* December 2000.

Grove, Lloyd. "Uma Up Close." *Harper's Bazaar.* November 2000.

Heath, Chris. "Portrait of a Trash-Talking Lady." *Rolling Stone.* April 13, 2000.

Jensen, Jeff. "Queen of Hearts." *Entertainment Weekly.* April 21, 2000.

Lonstein, Shoshanna. "Shoshanna Shares the Secrets of Her Success." *Cosmopolitan.* June 1999.

InStyle. "Cause Celeb." December 1999.

Marin, Rick. "Getting Over Gwyneth." *Harper's Bazaar.* February 2000.

Morrison, Toni. "The World According to Toni Morrison." *Essence.* May 1995.

O'Neill, Anne-Marie, et al. "Sarah Jessica Parker—Naughty but Nice." *People.* October 2, 2000.

People. "Pop Quiz with Katie Couric." March 20, 2000.

People. "Parting Words" (excerpt of Billie Jean King's commencement address to University of Massachusetts at Amherst). May 21, 2000, June 1, 2000.

People. "Brandi Chastain." December 31, 1999.

Reed, Susan. "The Champions." *Women's Sports and Fitness.* March 2000.

Rogers, Patrick. "Class Act: NY's Fairy Godmother Brooke Astor." *People.* August 24, 1998.

Rosenberg, Debra, and Michael Hirsh. "Chelsea's New Morning." *Newsweek.* April 3, 2000.

Stasio, Marilyn. "Emma Thompson: The World's a Stage." *On the Issues.* Fall 1998.

Taylor-Fleming, Anne. "The Battles of Billie Jean King." *Women's Sports and Fitness.* September 1998.

Williams, Patricia J. "Anita Hill's Second Act." *Harper's Bazaar.* October 1997.

Woodson, Michelle. "Jane Kisses 'Today' Goodbye." *Entertainment Weekly.* December 22, 1995.

Newspapers

Chicago Tribune, February 6, 1985.

[New York] *Daily News,* October 2, 1999.

New York Observer, September 25, 2000.

New York Post, September 19, 1999.

New York Times, January 22, 1994.

acknowledgments

WE GRATEFULLY thank our editor, Amy Hundley, for accompanying us on the journey of this book. She showed infinite patience, was either gentle or blunt when necessary, and coped graciously with the difficulties of working with a bicoastal writing team. Our deepest gratitude to our wonderful agent, Helen Breitweiser, who has always "gotten" this book and was the quintessence of equanimity and support throughout; she is a true friend. Many thanks to Morgan Entrekin for having faith in our book, and to Judy Hottensen and Charles Woods for their valuable input.

Thank you to Franco Wright and Adam Eastwood for designing a great website, without which we would have never been able to reach as many ladies as we did.

Thank you very much to all the ladies who responded to our survey. In particular, we are grateful to those who gave us the lengthy responses that provided us with such thoughtful quotations: Nicole Alger, Tamara Battle, Monica Bisgard, Adriana Brad, Pamela Caffray, Mary Cardell, Vanessa DelFabbro, Erica

Dunn, Elizabeth Endress, Rebecca Fabiano, Audrey Franks, Dana Fowler, Dana Galley, Celina Gerbic, Amy Grant, Beth Hafner, Kearney Harrington, Michaela Hellman, Fatima Johnson, Jean Kelly, Arianna Koransky, Tracey MacNeill, Sarah Maizes, Alanna Marks, Erin McMeekin, Donna Moore, Madeleine Pettey, Candice Proctor, Clare Roberts, Ellen Rooney, Amy Silk, Amy Smith, Paige St. John, Nicole Sullivan, Amy Tardio, and Heidi Zighera.

Thank you to the wonderful ladies who took the time out of their busy lives to be interviewed: Candice Bergen, Shoshanna Lonstein, Julianna Margulies, Liz Smith, Lesley Stahl, Linda Stasi, and Paula Zahn.

Noelle

Thank you to John Burke for his love, support, affection, and patience; John and Romina for loving me and putting up with my sometimes preachy big-sister ways; Alex Nhancale for being a true and wonderful friend; and Steven Rosato for being the paragon of generosity and goodness in an otherwise cynical world. And many, many thanks to Samantha Smith—a dear friend, a great editor at large, and a bona fide lady.

Dini

Thank you to the ladies who have been sounding boards and advisers throughout, including: Heidi Bettini, Alex Kuczynski, Sherri Rifkin, Mary Alice Sherrill, and Paige St. John. To Jasmine

Nielsen for the grace she shows me. To the fusilli heads, who have been there from the start; thank you to Julianna and Elizabeth. To my family, whose support is always sustaining. And an enormous thank-you to the remarkable lady who makes my life livable through the incredible care she gives: Janice Mills.